Natural
Pain Relief

Eliminate your aches and pains the natural way
Become pain free, feel better, and live longer

Natural
Pain Relief

Eliminate your aches and pains the natural way
Become pain free, feel better, and live longer

By Kevin Trudeau

Natural Pain Relief

This edition published by Natural Press, LLC
For information, address:

Natural Press, LLC
PO Box 8568
Pueblo, CO 81001

ISBN 13: 978-0-9911782-2-3
Interior design: The Printed Page, Phoenix, AZ

Manufactured in the United States of America

10 9 8 7 6 5 4 3 2 1

First Version

The information in this book was written and is intended for educational purposes only and should not be considered medical advice or counsel. If you have questions about your health, consult your physician and don't use this book as a substitute for needed medical help.

Table of Contents

Big Pharma's Pain Pill Addiction Trap

You are a target. Whether you realize it or not, whether you want to believe it or not, you have been targeted by one of the richest corporate industries in the world—the pharmaceutical manufacturers. Big Pharma wants your money and your devotion. Their path to prosperity is paved with your pain and your desire to end it.

We all know that dealing with pain is part of being human. Whether mild or severe, it's a symptom, a warning sign that something is wrong in our body and damage is being done. If we ignore it, or fail to treat it properly, we run the risk of developing a chronic pain condition which will make life miserable and, quite possibly, hasten our death.

Your first response to pain may usually be to try and eliminate it quickly using the most potent remedy available. That's where Big Pharma weighs in and grabs your attention with its claims for 'magic bullet' painkillers. But there is a really big downside to this approach. Reaching for 'high ballistic bullets' to produce a quick fix every time you feel an ache, or a twinge, or a pain that won't go away on its own amounts to a prescription for becoming a medical statistic, because addiction is what dependence on Big Pharma brings us as one of its many side effects.

Their path to prosperity is paved with your pain and your desire to end it.

Remember Celebrex, marketed for arthritis pain? How about Bextra, sold for pain and inflammation? Or the painkiller Vioxx? Big Pharma would like you to forget about those disasters. The drugs made billions of dollars for Big Pharma before the casualty figures of injuries and deaths among those taking the drugs caused them to be withdrawn from circulation. As if that wasn't outrage enough, it turns out those drugs were no more effective at relieving pain "than the aspirin in your medicine cabinet," and all the while, they were "killing thousands of us by causing heart attacks and stroke," observed biochemist Dr. Shawn M. Talbott, who has studied Big Pharma's shameful mortality record.

The latest looming pain drug scandal involves the chemical acetaminophen, which is used in both prescription and over-the-counter brand names including Vicodin, Percocet, and Tylenol. Taking too much of a pain reliever containing this chemical can lead to liver failure or death, cautioned the U.S. Food and Drug Administration in an early 2014 health warning to consumers. So how much is too much? More than 325 milligrams says this government agency. And yet, one gel tablet of Extra Strength Tylenol contains 500 milligrams, according to the label. Is it being pulled from the shelves as a health hazard? Nope. The FDA said it won't address over-the-counter products containing acetaminophen until it takes regulatory action at some unspecified date.

"Acetaminophen overdose is one of the most common poisonings worldwide," warned the U.S. National Institutes of Health. These poisonings occur more frequently when consumers take more than once acetaminophen product at a time, or drink alcoholic beverages while taking the products. So how long do we have to wait, how many of us have to be injured or killed, before our government takes action to hold Big Pharma truly and completely accountable?

As you can probably guess, it's being left up to you, the consumer, to exercise caution and restraint to prevent injury and death to yourself and your loved ones. For many of you, especially if you have heightened sensitivity to the chemicals in pain drugs, trying out natural pain relief alternatives is not just an option, it's a necessity.

There are other concerns we need to address surrounding pain drug use. Research shows that when left untreated, chronic pain can trigger severe depression. It's been estimated that one-third of all the people in this country will experience a bout with chronic pain at some point in their lives. It's the most common cause of work days lost and long term disability.

But keep in mind that depression can also occur while you are taking Big Pharma's painkillers because some of them have been documented to trigger mood disorders. That sets in motion a whole new cycle of prescription drug use to deal with this deteriorating mental and emotional condition. Each of these drugs present additional health risks to you with their own set of toxic side effects and long term consequences. It really is a vicious cycle and once you're caught up in it, it's a challenge to get off.

Nor should we forget that non-prescription over-the-counter pain relief drugs also carry risks for serious side effects to organs other than just your liver. Whether it's Tylenol, Advil, or Aleve, if you use them too long or use them in too high a dose in an attempt to relieve your pain, you can suffer injury to your stomach, kidneys, even your skin. So the best advice is to never take safety as a given when it comes to any kind of pharmaceuticals, particularly the pain reliever class of drugs.

You may already be asking yourself, do I really have effective and affordable alternatives to Big Pharma's medicine cabinet? Yes, indeed you do. That's why I wrote this book. You've got many more natural, proven remedies available for the entire scale of pain severity conditions than you may have ever imagined. These aren't New Age woo woo remedies. They are tried and proven substances from Nature and techniques produced by the genius of human ingenuity and as a result of patient observation using trial and error.

Four Good Reasons To Use Natural Pain Remedies

✔ You can become addicted to pharmaceutical pain pills.
✔ You can die from using pharmaceutical pain pills.
✔ Pharmaceutical pain pills are more costly than natural remedies.
✔ Natural pain remedies have proven effective in medical studies.

Don't believe it?

Choose not to believe it?

Just try to keep an open mind, if you can, for a few more pages.

Let's briefly examine the evidence.

1. **You can become addicted to pharmaceutical pain pills.**

   Addiction can happen to you. It can happen to anyone. Just ask any of the millions of people throughout the U.S. and the world who have already battled life-threatening dependencies formed by taking some of Big Pharma's highly addictive pain drugs.

Our own White House Office on Drug Control Policy has designated prescription painkiller drugs as "the nation's fastest-growing drug problem." The Physicians for Responsible Opioid Prescribing even conceded that more than one-quarter of all folks using opioid painkiller prescriptions have already become addicted.

Opioids are that class of synthetic and semi-synthetic drugs resembling morphine or related opiates (opium) in their effects, and include Oxycodone (marketed under the brand names OxyContin or Oxecta), Oxymorphone, Hydromorphone, and at least a dozen others all with different brand names. The most common reported side effects, besides their potential for addiction, are nausea, vomiting, drowsiness, headaches, and constipation. Those are just the less serious side effects. As a class of drugs they are considered most effective in dealing with pain associated with terminal cases of cancer, which is certainly understandable. It's their use in treating the entire range of other non-life- threatening ailments that creates a host of problems for individuals and society.

Physicians in the U.S. write millions of OxyContin pre-scriptions every year, particularly to treat arthritis and back pain. It used to be called 'Hillbilly heroin' because of its user popularity in rural areas of the Appalachian Mountains. What physicians soon found, as reported by *Fortune* in 2011, was that their "patients would crash, needing more and higher doses. Patients who took moderate amounts for backaches or arthritis could find themselves hooked."

You might recall that during the trial of singer Michael Jackson's personal physician it was revealed that Jackson had been taking high doses of the opioid painkiller Demerol. Expert witnesses testified that six weeks of high dose use by Jackson was enough to cause addiction and this may have contributed to his death.

The most tragic victims of painkiller addiction are the most defenseless,—infants and children. Through no fault of their own, they can become addicted in the womb if their mother is a chronic abuser of Big Pharma's pain medications during pregnancy. After being born, these toddlers experience the entire range of drug withdrawal symptoms from seizures to irritability, sweating, and body aches. Thousands of such sad cases have been noted by hospitals and other medical institutions around the nation.

Still another serious problem caused by the widespread prevalence of pain pill use comes in the costs to society from property crimes and violent robberies committed by pain pill addicts. In some regions of the country law enforcement authorities estimate that two-thirds of property theft crimes are the work of addicts trying to support their pain pill dependence. The same holds true for pharmacy robberies. It's not uncommon anymore to read of gun-wielding addicts shooting or even killing pharmacy employees while robbing them of hydrocodone (the main ingredient in Vicodin) and other prescription painkillers, such as Percocet.

2. **You can die from using pharmaceutical pain pills.**

It's no exaggeration to say that dependency and death are real consequences of reliance on pharmaceutical pain relievers. Statistics from the U.S. Centers for Disease Control and Prevention reveal how our nation's love affair with Big Pharma's pain pills has become a death pact, particularly over the past decade. More than 15,000 people in the U.S. die from prescription painkillers every year. Just among OxyContin and Vicodin users, who are primarily middle-aged men, fatal overdoses tripled during the first decade of the 21st century.

Don't believe for a moment this is a problem only being experienced by residents of the United States. Opioid prescription related deaths are rapidly increasing in Australia, Canada, and Britain, according to an August 2011 article in the *British Medical Journal.* It's a contagion in every developed country where Big Pharma has seized control of the pain relief marketplace.

The *Los Angeles Times* summed up the painkiller addiction epidemic and the resulting deaths this way in a September 2011 article: "The seeds of the problem were planted more than a decade ago by well-meaning efforts by doctors to mitigate suffering, as well as aggressive sales campaigns by pharmaceutical manufacturers."

3. **Pharmaceutical pain pills are more costly than natural remedies.**

How much do we Americans spend on pain remedies each year? At least $635 billion (yes, BILLION) annually, or about $2,000 for every human in the nation, and that is a conservative estimate according to a 2011 report by the Institute of Medicine.

Chronic pain conditions (chronic meaning lasting more than 60 days) are said to affect 100 million adult Americans. The leading causes of pain and pain medication use, says the National Institutes of Health, are low back pain (27% of survey respondents interviewed) followed by severe headache or migraines (15% of survey respondents). At least 20% of American adults (that is, 42 million ordinary folks) reported that pain disrupted their sleep each month.

Consumer Reports (August 2013) provided a pricing list for many of the most common prescription pain and sleep drugs:

- Nexium (for heartburn and acid reflux) $241 a month for a daily supply of 20-mg pills.

- Lunesta (for insomnia) $149 for 15 1-mg doses.

- Sumatriptan (for migraine headaches) $14 per 50-mg pill.

- Celebrex (for joint pain) $190 a month for a daily 200-mg pill.

To get 60 tablets (20-mg) of OxyContin you must pay nearly $300 at most pharmacies. The street value of these pills on the black market can reach $60 or more per pill for the higher dosages.

A *Time* magazine investigation of why prescription drugs cost so much concluded: "The prices Americans pay for prescription drugs, which are far higher than those paid by citizens of any other developed country, help explain why the pharmaceutical industry is—and has been for years—the most profitable of all businesses in the U.S."

By contrast, as you will discover throughout this book, most natural remedies for pain relief can be obtained for free, or will cost you very little compared to pharmaceutical drugs. As our nation tries to lower its overall health care costs and control prescription drug spending, one good place to start is with an emphasis on replacing expensive pharmaceuticals with less costly natural remedies, which have the added benefit of having far fewer side effects.

4. **Natural pain remedies have proven effective in medical studies.**

Big Pharma would rather you didn't know the extent to which mainstream medical science has demonstrated in laboratory study settings the effectiveness of many natural, non-synthetic and non-invasive remedies for managing pain. If more people knew, if more people successfully broke free of the 'magic bullet' pain pill spell, there would be a plunge in those huge pharmaceutical profits.

These natural substances and techniques for pain relief vary widely from using your mind to control pain signals being sent from your body, to using herbs and foods which provide your body with the nutrients it needs to prevent pain before it starts and to manage pain if and when it begins. Some of these natural remedies were discovered by ancient cultures and tribal societies, often by watching what animals in the wild use when sick or in pain. Their effectiveness and lack of serious side effects have been documented through trial and error over the course of thousands of years and have now been confirmed in peer-reviewed studies by teams of medical science researchers.

For example, did you know that cinnamon is one of 67 medicinal herbs in use throughout India since about 4,500 years ago to ease stomach pain and stomach distress? Only in our present day did medical science discover what the ancient healers of India already intuitively knew—the oil in cinnamon has antimicrobial properties, according to Daniel Mowrey, Ph.D., a plant medicine scientist who wrote *The Scientific Validation of Herbal Medicine*. Some modern toothpaste manufacturers had the good sense to add cinnamon to their products to help prevent tooth pain by preventing gum disease and tooth decay.

Yoga is an ancient practice involving a series of body postures (asanas) that range from the easy to perform to the more physically challenging. Who knew for hundreds of years, besides yoga practitioners, that certain gentle yoga positions could be effective in treating chronic lower back pain? Doing a posture called the half-cobra, for instance, which consists of lying flat on your stomach and then slowly lifting yourself up on your elbows, can reduce pain while strengthening the muscles that generate lower back pain. Many chiropractors now routinely recommend this and other related yoga postures to their pain patients.

Cinnamon and yoga are but two of the many dozens of non-drug pain remedies I am sharing with you in the pages of this book. These remedies were collected from medical authorities and research studies done throughout the world and represent the best and most up-to-date information that could be found.

In this book you will find nature's medicine chest of techniques and nondrug substances. Many of them are little publicized, yet well documented, and should give you pain relief for a wide assortment of ailments, from acid reflux, arthritis, and headaches, to menstrual cramps, muscle pain, and shingles.

> In this book you will find nature's medicine chest of techniques and nondrug substances.

By using these techniques and substances, especially in various combinations to create healing synergies, you will reduce your dependence on addictive painkillers and end your exposure to their many well-documented serious side effects. You will also be saving yourself a lot of money that would otherwise further fatten up the already rich pharmaceutical companies.

As an added bonus, I am providing you with a lot of useful information on nondrug remedies for insomnia and poor sleep, because a good night's sleep is the first casualty of chronic pain.

Without restful sleep, we weaken our body's immune system and become susceptible to more ailments faster than we do when getting the proper amount of sleep each night. It's another one of those vicious cycles. Pain = poor sleep = more pain = worse sleep or no sleep. Add pain drugs and sleep drug medications to the mix with all of their noxious side effects and you have a recipe for total health breakdown.

My wish for you, the reader, is that the information provided in this book will help guide you to living a pain-free life. Folks, you deserve it. You deserve good health and peace of mind. You no longer need to be a wage slave to addictive, costly drugs. You hold in your hands a passport for a journey that will change your experience of life for the better.

PART ONE

Pain Begins and Ends In Your Mind

24 Types of Pain Treatable With Natural Remedies

No matter what the source of the pain you experience, whether it's a headache or something more serious like a burn or fibromyalgia, the sensation you feel is in your brain. It's that organ which receives the pain signals from throughout your body and makes you aware of the injury or bodily dysfunction.

Let's say you burn your finger. Physical receptors connected to nerves in your finger communicate this burn sensation information up your arm and into your spinal cord. From the spinal cord this burn information shoots up into your brain and that is where the sensation of "feeling pain" is recorded.

What pain remedies are intended to do is to numb or short-circuit those pain signals being received in your brain. That's true whether the remedy is a natural practice or technique, a natural substance, or a prescribed pharmaceutical drug or an over-the-counter drug. Endorphins are your body's natural painkiller hormone and many of the techniques I will describe are designed to trigger the release of your own pain fighting guardians.

Mental or emotional upheaval in your life or constant stress can also cause a type of pain sensation in your body that is psychosomatic. You've probably heard the expression 'it's all in your mind.' This is true for psychosomatic illness, though the pain feels very real to the person afflicted with it. The phenomenon of psychosomatic pain reveals how powerful the human mind is in having a direct impact on the body. In turn, these 'mind-over-matter' effects can be harnessed in the healing process to turn off the pain circuits.

If the pain sensation, whatever its origin, doesn't go away on its own, or doesn't respond over time to natural or synthetic remedies, it's important to have a physician help you to isolate the cause of that pain before it becomes a more serious threat to your health. That backache, or jaw pain, or chest pain may be an indicator that cancer, or a stroke, or a heart attack, may be in your future.

As I noted in the Introduction, those of you who have developed a reliance on Big Pharma's drugs for treating pain face two life-altering repercussions: developing dependency or physical addiction with the possibility of death from an overdose, and a range of other side-effects (just read the warning labels) which can damage your liver and other body organs and shorten your life.

✔ Wouldn't you rather try a natural approach to treating pain without the drug use side effects or possible addiction?

✔ Wouldn't you rather dramatically cut the costs of treating your pain by using the much less expensive option of natural remedies?

✔ Wouldn't you like to stop fattening up the already rich pharmaceutical companies with your hard-earned money?

Sure, you might respond, but you still have questions or doubts. Are these natural remedies effective? Will they eliminate my pain? Or at the very least, will they enable me to manage the pain if it's a chronic condition?

Any concerns you may have about the effectiveness of natural remedies should be answered by the medical science research I have collected and cited with detail in this book. You will find listed and described in these pages an entire arsenal of pain-treating natural substances and techniques which have been subjected to rigorous scrutiny and testing by some of the leading physicians and scientists from throughout the world.

> These natural pain remedies can be divided into two broad categories: foods and herbs... and mental and physical techniques or practices...

Some of these natural remedies are little known. Others have been time-tested by tribal and ancient cultures. Still more natural remedies are recent discoveries affirmed in laboratory testing. Taken together, what these various and diverse natural approaches to pain offer you is an entire medicine chest as a practical and safe alternative to Big Pharma and its dangerous drugs.

These natural pain remedies can be divided into two broad categories: foods and herbs with substances which contain pain relieving nutrients; and mental and physical techniques or practices which help to interrupt pain signals to the brain and help you to better manage your pain condition. Many of the recommendations in these two categories also have the added benefit of helping to prevent certain types of pain from occurring in the first place.

To give you just a few examples of what you will learn about in more detail, take the ancient Chinese practice of Tai Chi. While Tai Chi's health benefits mostly revolve around stress relief, which helps in fighting pain, medical science has been busy testing all of the claims made about its healing effects. Among the study findings so far: Tai Chi lowers cardiovascular disease risk, reduces blood pressure and total cholesterol levels, heightens motor skills in Parkinson's disease patients, relieves tension headaches, creates antibody immunity to shingles, enhances the protective antibody activity of vaccines, increases bone mineral density in post-menopausal women, contributes to rehabilitation in stroke victims, and has beneficial effects on blood in Type 2 diabetic patients.

Or consider what the blue-green alga called Spirulina can do for you. As a dietary supplement studies have shown it to be useful in treating everything from Alzheimer's disease to hypertension, stroke, and cataracts. This isn't just pond scum we're talking about, folks. This is one of Nature's most useful health bounties for humankind's benefit. In the pain realm it's been documented as a treatment for arthritis, fibromyalgia, ulcers, and many types of inflammation.

So, has your physician recommended algae supplements or that you take up the practice of Tai Chi? I imagine the answer is probably not unless you are fortunate enough to have found a naturopathic physician. Too many mainstream doctors are still so enamored with drugs and so brainwashed by the marketing of Big Pharma that researching and recommending natural alternatives hasn't even occurred to them.

The one natural pain remedy that everyone on the planet should be familiar with, the one that mainstream physicians have no trouble recommending, is aspirin, an extract of willow bark. It's been a pain remedy for many hundreds of years.

When the explorers Lewis and Clark embarked on their epic journey through the West in 1803, they carried with them willow bark extract to treat fever and lessen pain-related injuries. It was the natural wonder drug of its day. Then the drug and dye firm Bayer patented the extract in 1899 and the product known as 'aspirin' was launched to dominate the pain relief consumer market. You don't see anyone walking around chewing willow bark anymore. (Bayer also manufactured and distributed heroin as a painkiller the year before aspirin was introduced.)

Those were the days just before the widespread emergence of pharmaceutical companies and their fixation on 'better-living-through-chemistry' synthetic drugs. Had those companies turned their attention way back then to developing natural pain fighting herbs from the Amazon, from tribal cultures, and perfecting the use of 'folk' remedies, instead of developing and mass producing endless lines of synthetic drugs, there might not have been reason for me to be writing this book for you today.

Perhaps the greatest weapon in your pain-fighting arsenal is your own mind. You will learn about many mind practices which you can use to assist the foods and herbs and various physical techniques in creating synergies to trigger, magnify, and accelerate your healing process. Try combinations of these safe, non-invasive and relatively inexpensive natural remedies for the best results in easing your pain symptoms.

Pain isn't something you must resign yourself to endure. It's something to be managed, if not entirely vanquished. Now you have in your hands the tools to do that naturally without reason to fear the onset of side effects.

✔ It's time to stop letting the pharmaceutical industry define your pain relief choices.

✔ It's time to take responsibility for your own health and your own pain relief.

✔ It's time to try new approaches so pain no longer distorts and shapes your experience of life.

Acid Reflux

It's a condition called Gastroesophageal Reflux Disease that occurs when a backwash of stomach acid irritates the lining of your esophagus causing pain and other symptoms, such as heartburn. It's considered a disease rather than just an annoying condition when these symptoms occur twice or more a week. That is according to research provided by Mayo Clinic.

Among the conditions Mayo physicians say can increase your risk of GERD:
✔ Obesity
✔ Hiatal hernia
✔ Pregnancy
✔ Smoking
✔ Dry mouth
✔ Asthma
✔ Diabetes
✔ Delayed stomach emptying
✔ Connective tissue disorders, such as scleroderma
✔ Zollinger-Ellison syndrome

Recommended lifestyle changes include avoiding foods that you determine are resulting in acid reflux and avoiding any food two hours before going to bed. Fatty and fried foods are two of the biggest culprits causing acid reflux, along with tomato sauce, alcohol, and caffeine.

An X-ray or an endoscopy test looking down your throat may be required to properly diagnose the disease and its severity. Physicians often prescribe drugs called proton pump inhibitors such as Nexium. Severe cases of GERD may require surgery. Less severe cases and the pain associated with it can be treated with natural remedies.

Here are some natural remedies for GERD and less severe conditions of acid reflux as provided by Mayo Clinic:

Herbal remedies. Among the herbal remedies sometimes used are **licorice, slippery elm, chamomile, and marshmallow.** It's important to note some of these herbals may interfere with medications you are taking, so be sure to ask your physician about safe dosages.

Relaxation therapies. Techniques to calm your levels of stress and anxiety may reduce some of the signs and symptoms of GERD. Among these relaxation techniques considered useful are **progressive muscle relaxation and guided imagery.**

Acupuncture. Acupuncture, which involves inserting thin needles into specific points on your body, has study evidence behind it that it helped people with heartburn that had persisted despite the use of medication.

Arthritis
(Basal joint; Gout; Osteoarthritis; Rheumatoid)

It's a word you're probably very familiar with, but are you aware of all the different types of arthritis? Here are some of them.

Basal joint arthritis: It's in your thumb and occurs when the cartilage wears away in your thumb joint. Your entire hand can swell up from it. The strength and range of motion in your thumb becomes diminished and that makes it difficult to open anything like a doorknob. It most commonly occurs in women aged 40 years and above. As an alternative to drugs and surgery, Mayo Clinic specialists advise that you:

1. Improve your joint's mobility by doing daily range of **motion exercises** moving your thumb around in a circular motion;

2. Alternate immersing your thumb in **heat and then cold** each day to reduce the swelling and relax the joint.

Gouty arthritis: If you've ever had a sudden pain and burning attack in the joint of your big toe, the most common area for gout, you remember the sensation well. You think your big toe has been set on fire from the inside and even the weight of a sheet pressing on it can feel unbearable. It mostly happens to men. It can occur not just in the big toe joint, but in your wrists, hands, ankles, and knees. A high level of uric acid in your blood can trigger gout by forming urate crystals in your joints. Too much alcohol can cause it, so can some prescription medications for high blood pressure.

As alternative treatments if you want to bypass prescription drugs:

1. Try eating **cherries** and drinking **cherry juice**, which is known to lower uric acid levels in the body.

2. **Blueberries, blackberries, and raspberries** may also help. Drink copious amounts of pure water.

3. Also use **breathing exercise and meditation** to help with the pain.

   (For more detail about natural remedies for Gout pain, see the separate listing for it later in this section.)

Osteoarthritis: As the protective cartilage located on the ends of your bones wear out with age, any joint in your body can be affected, though the most common areas are in your hips, knees, lower back, neck, and hands. It usually gets worse with age. Pain will become more intense with movement. Flexibility and range of movement in the joint will diminish. Stiffness in the joint, particularly when getting up in the morning, will become more apparent. Women get this degenerative disease more frequently than men.

Anti-inflammatory drugs and even narcotics are typically prescribed for osteoarthritis, along with physical therapy and even in the worst cases, joint replacement surgery.

Natural remedies, as identified by Mayo Clinic, to manage osteoarthritis pain include:

1. Gentle but regular **exercise** and losing weight.

2. Alternating joint exposure to **heat and cold** to relieve stiffness and pain.

3. Nondrug **heat creams** which numb the pain when rubbed on.

4. **Acupuncture**, shown to benefit folks suffering from knee osteoarthritis.

5. **Glucosamine and chondroitin**, nutritional supplements, may be helpful to some people.

6. **The positive effects of Tai Chi and yoga**, demonstrated in some studies to reduce the severity of pain associated with osteoarthritis.

   (For more detail about natural remedies for Osteoarthritis pain, see the separate listing for it later in this section.)

Rheumatoid arthritis: This chronic inflammatory disorder usually affects the lining of the small joints in your hands and feet. Your immune system has mistakenly attacked your own body tissues to cause it. It usually affects women more than men and typically develops beyond 40 years of age. As with other types of arthritis the joints become stiff and tender, but in addition there is fatigue and small bumps of tissue which form under the skin of the arms.

Both steroids and non-steroidal anti-inflammatory drugs are typically prescribed by physicians as well as medications for the immune system. Surgery can also be used to repair damaged joints.

Natural remedies identified by Mayo Clinic to manage Rheumatoid arthritis pain include:

1. **Regular gentle exercise** to strengthen muscles around the joints.

2. Alternating **heat and cold** to relax the affected body areas.

3. Reduce stress in your life (stress exacerbates the condition) using **Hypnosis, Guided imagery, Deep breathing**, and other relaxation techniques shown in studies to be effective in controlling pain.

4. Seed oils of **Evening Primrose, Black Currant, and Borage** contain fatty acids helpful in reducing stiffness and pain.

5. **Fish oil supplements** may also be helpful in pain and stiffness reduction.

6. The gentle stretches and exercises of **Tai Chi** to combat pain accompanying rheumatoid arthritis.

    (For more detail about natural remedies for Rheumatoid arthritis pain, see the separate listing for it later in this section.)

Other Natural Remedies for Arthritis Pain

✔ **Mindfulness**: To assess the effect of Mindfulness-Based Stress Reduction on symptoms associated with rheumatoid arthritis, 31 people attended an eight-week Mindfulness course and 32 others who had no exposure to Mindfulness became the control group.

Result: Researchers reported: "At 6 months there was significant improvement in psychological distress and well-being, and marginally significant improvement in depressive symptoms" in the Mindfulness group, as opposed to the control group, and "a 35% reduction in psychological distress among those treated." October 2007, *Arthritis Rheumatism*.

✔ **Algae, Spirulina**: Spirulina in concentrated supplement form was used in a series of studies to test its anti-inflammatory potential against pain crippling arthritic conditions.

Result: In tests of spirulina on arthritic lab animals it was found that the substance "significantly normalizes to near normal conditions" and thus it has "promising protection efficacy against collagen-induced arthritis." June 2009, *Inflammopharmacology.*

Result: In another study the scientists explained "the anti-arthritic effect exerted by Spirulina" as partly due to the "anti-inflammatory and antioxidative properties of its constituent, phycocyanin." April 2002, *Mediators Inflammation*.

✔ **Avocado and Soybean** supplementation: Numerous studies have demonstrated the usefulness of the unsaponifiables found in soybeans and avocados in treating the symptoms of osteoarthritis and also in preventing the disease.

Result: "The majority of rigorous trial data available to date suggest that avocado/soybean unsaponifiables is effective for the symptomatic treatment of osteoarthritis." October 2003, *Clinical Rheumatology*.

Another Result: "Basic scientific research studies and a systematic review and meta-analysis of the available high-quality randomized clinical trials indicate that 300 mg. of avocado and soybean unsaponifiables per day (with or without glucosamine and chondoritin sulfate) appears to be beneficial for patients with hip or knee osteoarthritis." June 2010, *Physical Sportsmedicine*.

✔ **Curcumin**: You probably know it as the Indian spice in curries. Just over the past decade a lot of research has shown it to be a potent natural treatment for dozens of ailments, including arthritic conditions.

Result: "The large numbers of inexpensive natural products that can modulate inflammatory responses, but lack side effects, constitute 'goldmines' for the treatment of arthritis. Numerous agents derived from plants can suppress cell signaling intermediates, including **curcumin, resveratrol, cranberries and peanuts, tea polyphenols, genistein, quercetin from onions, silymarin from artichoke**." June 2007, *Current Opinion Pharmacology*.

✔ **Garlic**: Sulfur compounds isolated from common household garlic have proven effective in having anti-inflammatory and anti-arthritic effects in the human body. Supplementation is recommended since the amount of garlic you would need to eat to get the same results would mean huge helpings of garlic at every meal.

Result: "The present results suggested that thiacremonone {a sulfur compound isolated from garlic} exerted its anti-inflammatory and anti-arthritic properties…and thus could be a useful agent for the treatment of inflammatory and arthritic diseases." September 2009, *Arthritis Research Therapy*.

✔ **Olive oil**: A key component of the Mediterranean diet, which has proven to have numerous health benefits, olive oil contains natural chemicals which studies say can be used to treat both osteoarthritis and rheumatoid arthritis.

Result: "This class of molecules from olecanthal isolated from extra virgin olive oil was found to display nonsteroidal anti-inflammatory drug activity similar to that of ibuprofen and thus shows potential as a therapeutic weapon for the treatment of inflammatory degenerative joint diseases such as osteoarthritis." June 2010, *Arthritis Rheumatology*.

Another Result: "Increased olive oil consumption is implicated in a reduction in rheumatoid arthritis. Olive oil intake also has been shown to modulate immune function, particularly the inflammatory processes associated with the immune system." December 2004, *Lipids*.

Back pain

If your back pain isn't related to an injury, chances are the pain may be due to weak or weakening back muscles. One of the worst things you can do under these circumstances is to stop exercising. Many back specialists recommend exercise, using flexibility training and gentle weight or resistance training, rather than just bed rest, to help heal the condition. One of those specialists is Dr. Leon Root, author of *Oh, My Aching Back,* who estimates that up to 90% of all back problems are due to weak back muscles.

The most common form of back pain is in the lower back and that can be the result of something so seemingly simply as poor posture or something unexpected like injury from falling off a ladder. Acute lower back pain can produce a debilitating condition requiring extended bed rest—you've heard the old expression, "my back went out." It's one of the most common reasons for missing work.

Herbal remedies for back pain were identified in the book, *The Green Pharmacy*, authored by James A. Duke, Ph.D., who oversaw the U.S. Department of Agriculture research lab investigating healing herbs from all over the world, particularly from the jungle rain forests of the Amazon. This expert on herbal healing traditions recommended these remedies:

- ✓ **Red Pepper (capsicum)**: The pain relieving chemical capsicum is found at high concentrations in the common spicy red pepper. A tiny amount of this chemical, according to Duke, "provides the active ingredient in some powerful pharmaceutical topical analgesics." Red pepper can be effective in treating pain both when it is eaten, and when it is mashed up and applied directly to the painful area of the back. It also triggers a release of your body's own pain-relieving endorphins. If you apply the mashed up red pepper to your skin, Duke advised that you place the mash into any white skin cream to make the application. Needless to say, if the cream irritates your skin you should discontinue its use.

- ✓ **White Willow**: Salicin in willow is an herbal aspirin and has been a natural pain reliever in use for more than 2,000 years. It might find its best use boiled as a tea, if you choose to take it that way. Another salicylate rich plant is wintergreen, and still another is birch bark, both in long use by Native American tribes that boiled and drank it, or applied it directly to the lower back as a pain reliever.

- ✓ **Peppermint and related mints**: The compounds camphor and menthol found in peppermint and other mints are often used in over-the-counter medications sold to treat pains in the back. These rubbing compounds can also be used on your own, each by them self or mixed together.

- ✓ **Essential Oils**: Duke lists **sage, rosemary, thyme, horse balm, and mountain dittany** as useful for treating the back spasms which trigger or intensify back pain because these plant oils contain carvacrol and thymol known to help your back muscles to relax. Just add a few drops of any of these oils to regular massage oil and massage the concoction into the painful area.

Aroma therapists also recommend using **lavender, black pepper, ginger, and birch oils** for back pain relief. Duke wrote that all of them contain lab-tested ingredients proven to be useful. They are more than just folklore. He also suggested that oils be used instead of over-the-counter products because the chemically isolated compounds don't work as well as when the oils have all of their ingredients interacting together. This is the concept of synergy at work and it's true as well for the beneficial foods we eat—the valuable nutrients that work together to boost our health aren't nearly as effective when they are isolated in pill or supplement form. In the case of the oils, as Duke pointed out, they evolved to "protect the plants from pests and other environmental stresses. The fact that aromatic herb oils evolved into a chemically complex mixture suggests that all the chemicals in them work together."

✔ **Vitamin B6, Tryptophan, Ginger**: These nutritional supplements may help you in easing your back pain, wrote Dr. Neal Barnard in his book, *Foods That Fight Pain*. In the case of the B vitamin, it has been used to treat carpal tunnel syndrome and is thought to be useful for back pain because it assists your body in developing pain resistance. A study published in the *Annals of the New York Academy of Science* found B vitamin supplements of up to 150 mg a day cut the back pain relapse rate by half over six months of use.

Tryptophan is an amino acid that helps to increase the amount of serotonin in your brain, and it is serotonin which is that natural brain chemical instrumental in pain control. A 1996 study in the journal *Advances in Pain Research Therapy* noted how supplements of this compound consistently reduced pain in a group of men with chronic back pain. Eating rice, pasta, and potatoes will naturally boost your levels of tryptophan.

Ginger is a common spice you are probably quite familiar with and while Dr. Barnard said evidence for its usefulness in back pain hasn't yet been demonstrated in clinical trials, it's worth trying because it is known to help in blocking inflammation in some musculoskeletal disorders.

Other Techniques for Back Pain

✔ **Dr. Sarno's Mind/Body Prescription**: What if your back pain really is 'all in your mind'? Can you accept that idea and then begin to treat the cause of your pain, not just your symptoms, while disregarding mainstream doctors who tell you that you need pharmaceutical drugs or even surgery? This may be a mind-boggling challenge for some folks. Can your mind accept that your mind is at fault?

If you can open your mind wide enough—without letting your brains (as in common sense) fall out—you may be ready for the ideas of Dr. John E. Sarno, MD, a retired professor of Clinical Rehabilitation Medicine at New York University School of Medicine. He was the first to describe and begin diagnosing a condition known as Tension Myositis Syndrome (TMS), which causes real physical symptoms such as chronic back pain even though there is no real structural abnormality in your body causing it. The pain results from a mild oxygen deprivation coming from your autonomic nervous system and that, in turn, results from accumulated stress and repressed emotions.

Anger and deep-seated resentments in the mind can build up over time, with direct effects on the body, resulting in the symptoms of pain in your back, shoulder, neck, and other parts of you. Additionally, Dr. Sarno believes that TMS is the cause of all sorts of common disorders such as irritable bowel syndrome, ulcers, asthma, prostatitis, headaches, etc. We all experience these unexpressed emotions in different ways, in different parts of our bodies, just as Dr. Sarno's techniques for treatment will work differently for each person. So each of us must identify which of his little or no cost techniques best suit us. That process begins with recognizing that we may be in control of this disorder. In fact, Dr. Sarno says that the vast majority of people will get better simply by *learning* about TMS and changing their perceptions of their pain. If you read Dr. Sarno's various books—*Mind Over Back Pain* and *Healing Back Pain: The Mind-Body Connection*—you will get a thorough description of how TMS is initiated and how you can go about treating it. If you want a quicker and more concise overview of his treatment ideas, go to www.tmswiki.org. On this website you will find TMS practitioners in your area. You will also be introduced to the basic self treatment concepts, along with a 6-week Structured Educational Program which includes many of the techniques presented in this natural pain remedy book, such as developing the important pain-reducing skills of meditation and deep breathing exercises.

Dr. Sarno's work has been subjected to medical study scrutiny. Here is a good example.

A team of six medical researchers worked with 51 patients who had chronic back pain and been diagnosed with tension myositis syndrome. The treatment interventions included written educational materials, a structured workbook (guided journal), educational audio CDs, and psychotherapy, in some cases. Follow-up examinations lasted up to a year after treatment.

Results: Pain decreased an average of 52% for those who had scored 'average' pain levels and 35% for those with the 'worst' pain level scores. Medication usage also significantly decreased as physical mobility increased. September 2007, *Alternative Therapies in Health and Medicine.*

✔ **Chiropractic Treatments**: One study in particular has contributed to a body of evidence showing that chiropractic manipulations of the back, especially the lower back, may help some people with back pain reduce the severity of their symptoms. In the 1995 study published in the *British Medical Journal,* 741 men and women aged 18 to 64 years were monitored over a period of three years after receiving either chiropractic manipulation of their lower back pain or having received hospital outpatient management. Those in the chiropractic group got more pain relief and more satisfaction in the long term than those who had regular hospital care.

Low Back Pain: Studies of spinal manipulation, cognitive behavioral therapy, massage, acupuncture, and yoga for low back pain treatment were collected as published through 2006 and compared and analyzed.

Results: "We found good evidence that cognitive behavioral therapy and spinal manipulation are all moderately effective for chronic or sub-acute low back pain. We found fair evidence that acupuncture, massage and yoga are also effective for chronic low back pain." October 2007, *Annals Internal Medicine.*

✔ **Osteopathic Manual Treatment**: By stretching and kneading the soft tissue around your inflamed back muscles, or by applying pressure at specific sites on your back, an osteopath seeks release where your muscle fibers are tight. In the *Annals* *of Family Medicine,* a 2013 study noted how 63% of patients with chronic lower back pain who, over the course of eight weeks, underwent six sessions of this manual treatment, experienced a 30% or greater lessening of pain discomfort, resulting in a sharply decreased need for painkillers.

✔ **Massage with Ice and Heat**: This is one of those common sense suggestions. Ice is a great pain reliever because it temporarily blocks pain signals and helps to reduce swelling. Ice packs or even bags of frozen corn or peas wrapped in cloth can be applied to the back. Follow that hours later with moist heat—getting inside a sauna would be great. Finally, getting a massage from your partner or from a massage therapist, with concentration on the aching area, is a guaranteed relaxer that also soothes the mind.

In a study assessing alternative medicine treatments for back pain a large team of researchers evaluated several hundred randomized controlled trial studies, one of them massage.

Results: "Massage was superior to placebo or no treatment in reducing pain and disability amongst subjects with acute/sub-acute low back pain. Massage was also significantly better than physical therapy in improving back pain." October 2010, *Evidence Reports/Technology Assessments.*

✔ **Stretching Exercises**: Another one of those common sense steps you can and probably should take is to do gentle stretching. Start while you are still in bed. While on your back, raise your arms and stretch them slowly over your head and gently pull your knees to your chest, one knee at a time. Release your arms and knees until you are stretched out again and repeat the entire process several more times. There are sets of other back pain exercises recommended by physical therapists which you will find described, photographed, and diagrammed if you do an Internet search under 'exercises for lower back pain'.

✔ **Yoga**: Combining exercise with stretching may be the best physical activity of all for chronic back pain, low back pain in particular. This can be a gentle yet effective way to build back muscle strength. Numerous studies have been done testing the proposition that yoga will help to relieve chronic low back pain and the results have been uniformly positive.

An examination of 10 randomized controlled trials of yoga involving 967 chronic low back pain patients found "strong evidence" for a short term effect on pain severity and "moderate evidence" for long term effects. Yoga also had no adverse effects on those who undertake it. May 2013, *Clinical Journal of Pain*.

✔ **Mindfulness**: A study of 37 adults aged 65 years and older, with moderate intensity back pain suffered daily, participated in an eight-week Mindfulness program with periodic assessments of pain, physical function, and quality of life. They used the program technique an average of 31 minutes a day, an average of four days a week under direction of the University of Pittsburgh's Department of Medicine.

Result: As the researchers reported, at the end of the intervention the group "displayed significant improvement" in the lowering of pain, in physical function, and overall quality of life. February 2008, the journal *Pain*.

✔ **Stress Management**: There is an important relationship between stress and pain. Whether back pain is the result of an accident, illness, surgery, or a progressive debilitating condition, stress management is essential to keep the pain from getting worse. Research has shown that people suffering from chronic pain have higher cortisol levels than healthy persons. Any technique which manages or reduces stress, be it meditation, mindfulness, cognitive behavioral therapy, or even self-hypnosis, is a useful adjunct for dealing with back pain in particular and any chronic pain. February 2013, *Brain*.

Birth Pain

If you're a woman who has given birth, you know how painful the act of bringing new life into the world can be, with or without pharmaceutical drug help. Many women have turned to natural practices, particularly mental focus and breathing techniques, as a primary or adjunct therapy for birth pain relief because they want to avoid narcotic pain relievers as much as possible.

✔ **Lamaze**: Perhaps the best known and most widely used natural childbirth technique, it teaches women methods for coping with extreme pain during labor. This natural birthing system involves learning to breathe through the pain and includes massage and spontaneous pushing. Some women who make the decision to give birth naturally do so because they fear that local anesthetics used by mainstream physicians might pose potential harm to themselves or to their newborn.

A review of the medical literature on the breathing exercises used in the Lamaze technique was conducted.

Result: "Controlled breathing enhances relaxation and decreases perception of pain. It is one of many comfort strategies taught in Lamaze classes. In restricted birthing environments, breathing may be the only non-pharma-cological comfort strategy available to women. Conscious breathing and relaxation, especially in combination with a wide variety of comfort strategies, can help women avoid unnecessary medical intervention and have a safe, healthy birth." Spring 2011, *Journal of Perinatal Education*.

Other Relaxation Techniques

✔ **Guided Imagery**: Using your imagination to see yourself relaxed can be a powerful and soothing mind tool. Soft music in the background may help. (For more information, see the section on Natural Techniques later in this book.)

✔ **Hypnosis**: Some of you are more hypnotizable than others, so this technique may not work equally well for everyone. Hypnosis can give you the feeling of being in control of your pain. Once you learn the technique you can use self-hypnosis to induce a pain control state of mind. (For more information, see the section on Natural Techniques.)

✔ **Massage**: Having your feet or hands simultaneously massaged as you enter labor can help to distract you from the pain and this soothing touch can help you release your own natural pain relief hormones.

✔ **Meditation**: By focusing your mind on repeating mantras or on the use of meditation techniques taught in Vipassana or other ancient meditation traditions, you can help yourself push the pain out so it isn't so much the focus of your awareness. (For more information, see the section on Natural Techniques.)

✔ **Reflexology**: Using this form of acupressure (which is related to acupuncture), pressure is applied to the soles of your feet prior to and during the childbirth process. (Read more on reflexology, acupressure, and acupuncture in the section on Natural Techniques.)

Diabetic Neuropathy

If you suffer from diabetes you may already have developed diabetic neuropathy, which is nerve damage to your legs and feet caused by high blood sugar. It can be a very painful condition.

You may experience both pain and numbness in your extremities along with other symptoms that show damage to your heart, urinary tract, and digestive system. Along with controlling your blood sugar and eating an overall healthy diet, which means lots of fruits and vegetables, there are a few other steps you can take to manage the pain and other symptoms.

The helpful physicians at Mayo Clinic offer these recommendations:

✔ **Stay active**. You need to keep exercising every day to whatever extent you can. Proper circulation of blood flow is important to healing and pain management. If your neuropathy is severe, you may need to do swimming or cycling to keep weight off your feet and legs as much as possible.

Alternative Treatments to Help Relieve Pain

✔ **Capsaicin**: This all-purpose pain remedy taken from hot peppers can reduce pain sensations in your feet and legs when rubbed on. There are capsaicin creams available in drug stores so you don't have to mix your own from scratch. These include Zostrix and ArthriCare.

✔ **Alpha-lipoic acid**: This antioxidant found in some foods is considered effective when used as a supplement for some people with neuropathy pain.

✔ **Acupuncture**: More than one session will be needed, but there are many reports that traditional Chinese acupuncture can help to lessen the severity of foot and leg pain associated with neuropathy.

✔ **Biofeedback**: By learning how to control some of your body responses to lessen pain, you can put this biofeedback device to work training you to have the same responses when you aren't hooked up to the machine.

✔ **Medical Marijuana**: An overview of numerous randomized controlled trials examining the use of cannabinoids (a marijuana compound) in treating neuropathic pain concluded that cannabinoids "are safe and modestly effective" as a pain treatment approach. November 2011, *British Journal of Clinical Pharmacology.*

Earache

Mostly occurring in children during their first five years of life, earaches are often due to an infection, though a build-up of ear wax may cause it, or a perforated eardrum, or a condition originating in your head or neck.

Aspirin is often effective for earaches but there are also herbs for adults that have been recommended by James A. Duke, Ph.D., perhaps the world's leading authority on healing herbs. Here are some of the herbal remedies he suggests:

✔ **Echinacea**: Antibiotic and immune system boosting have both been the primary benefits claimed for it; to use it, take a teaspoon of the dried herb and prepare it as a tea to drink three times a day.

✔ **Ephedra**: This Chinese herb contains ephedrine and pseudo-ephedrine as active ingredients. Duke notes how a study of frequent fliers found that 70% who took pseudoephedrine for recurrent ear pain did have relief of their symptoms.

✔ **Garlic**: Dripping garlic oil directly into your ears may sound a little creepy, but this eardrop, according to Dr. Duke, "has been shown to treat fungal infections as well or better than pharmaceutical drugs." (If you have a perforated eardrum, don't drip garlic oil or any other herbal eardrops into your ears.)

✔ **Goldenseal**: Described as a potent natural antibiotic, it is often used in combination (or mixed) with echinacea and licorice root. Use it as a tea.

✔ **Forsythia, Gentian, and Honeysuckle**: Combined together in powdered form as part of Chinese medicine, this antibiotic mixture can be used as a tea for earaches or can be sprinkled on food.

✔ **Teatree**: In Aromatherapy this antiseptic is usually applied to your skin, but you can mix a few drops of it with vegetable oil, wrote Duke, for eardrops. Do not under any circumstances consume Teatree. If taken internally, it can have poisonous effects. So beware!

Endometriosis

This often painful condition in women occurs when tissue lining the uterus begins to grow outside it, affecting the ovaries and bowel tissue. Pain can be severe, particularly during menstruation.

Symptoms of having endometriosis include chronic pelvic pain, pain during menstruation, bloating, fatigue, constipation or diarrhea, and pain experience during sexual intercourse. Some women even have the condition without these symptoms but, for the most part, pain is the common symptom denominator. One theorized cause for the upsurge in cases of endometriosis is exposure to the many estrogen-like synthetic chemicals that now surround us in the environment. (Estrogen stimulates cell growth.)

According to Mayo Clinic, risk factors for endometriosis include having never given birth, having a mother, aunt or sister with the condition, any history of pelvic infection, and any other medical conditions which obstruct normal menstrual flow.

A range of natural alternative treatments have been employed to enable women to manage the pain and other symptoms. Many of these treatments have been endorsed and promoted by the Endometriosis Foundation of America and include dietary and lifestyle changes, acupuncture, aromatherapy, chiropractic treatment, exercise, osteopathy, naturopathy, and healing herbs.

Lifestyle Remedies for Endometriosis Pain

- ✔ **Diet and Nutrition**: If you limit or cut out entirely your consumption of sugar, caffeine, carbohydrates, red meats, fast foods, processed foods, and food additives, many nutritionists believe you will help to relieve the pain associated with endometriosis and even help to prevent it from developing in the first place. It's also important to limit your intake of xenoestrogens from foods such as non-organic dairy products and meat products because anything non-organic often contains growth hormones which can magnify the impact of endometriosis.

  Dr. Neal Barnard, in his book *Foods That Fight Pain,* cited anecdotal evidence of women with endometriosis who adopted a lowfat vegetarian diet to balance their hormones. Within three months each of the women felt better, and within six months all of the pain associated with their condition disappeared. If they deviated from this diet by consuming dairy products or meat, the pain came charging back at them. While anecdotes don't constitute infallible evidence, they do show a pattern and the pattern in this instance is clear—dietary choices and habits play a distinct role in the onset of endometriosis and the treatment of symptoms, particularly the often debilitating pain.

- ✔ **Exercise**: You read this one throughout the book. Since exercise stimulates your release of endorphins, and endorphins help fight pain, and exercise also relieves stress which intensifies pain, why not embrace a daily exercise regimen to assist you in managing the pain you feel from endometriosis?

Let's briefly examine each of the natural remedies.

- ✔ **Acupuncture**: Because the use of this procedure may release endorphins, which are natural painkillers, into your blood stream, this could be useful in treating some instances of pain.

- ✔ **Aromatherapy**: Essential oils from certain plants may be effective for some women and include **sage, fennel, bergamont, cypress, and geranium.**

- ✔ **Chiropractic Treatment**: By correcting any dislocations in your musculoskeletal system, particularly in your lumbar spine and thoracic spine areas, you may receive some benefit helpful to eliminating part of the source of your pain. Osteopathy is another technique to try and it involves the manipulation of your muscles, bones, and ligaments to correct body problems which may contribute to endometriosis pain.

- ✔ **Herbs**: Among the herbs said by herbalists to be helpful in treating endometriosis and related pain symptoms are **cranberry, St. John's wort, blue cohosh, peppermint, valerian, evening primrose, red raspberry, yam, white willow.**

- ✔ **Soybeans**: This may sound counterintuitive after what you've read concerning estrogens and endometriosis, but various natural medicine authorities recommend soy products for treating the symptoms even though soybeans are high in two estrogen-like plant compounds—daidzein and genistein. These phytoestrogens, according to herb expert Dr. James A. Duke, crowd out the more harmful forms of estrogen circulating in your blood. Bean sprouts are another even healthier source of genistein for your diet. Pinto beans are still another source of genistein as well as daidzein.

✔ **Flax**: In flaxseed, lignans are compounds which are thought to be useful in preventing or treating endometriosis. Try eating bread containing flaxseeds and also using flaxseed oil when possible.

✔ **Natural progesterone**: In his analysis of natural substances to treat symptoms associated with endometriosis, Dr. Neal Barnard singled out natural progesterone as one strategy to balance out the effects of estrogen as a factor in endometriosis. Typically used from day eight to day 26 of a woman's monthly cycle, a two-ounce jar of natural progesterone is involved and continued for about four months. About 40 to 50 mg is used each day.

Fibromyalgia

Much more common among women than men, this musculoskeletal pain disorder is accompanied by sleep disruption, fatigue, and mood swings. "Researchers believe that fibromyalgia amplifies painful sensations by affecting the way your brain processes pain signals," according to Mayo Clinic.

A constant dull ache is how many fibromyalgia sufferers describe the sensation they feel in their muscles. Other pain is felt when pressure is applied to tender point locations, such as the inner knees, outer elbows, front sides of the neck, between the shoulder blades, and at the back of the head. What causes fibromyalgia remains a mystery, though some experts believe it is genetics combined with physical or emotional trauma which plays a causative role.

Generally a diagnosis of fibromyalgia comes if you experience widespread body pain lasting three months or more, or you feel pain at 11 or more of the 18 identified tender points for the ailment.

Lifestyle improvements which may help the condition include regular exercise, stress reduction, getting proper amounts of sleep, and eating healthy foods, which is to say lots of fruits and vegetables.

Mayo Clinic specialists recommend these natural treatments:

✔ **Acupuncture**, which some studies have shown may relieve pain symptoms in some patients, but not all.

In this review of studies done on acupoint stimulation (as done by acupuncture and acupressure), a total of 16 randomized clinical trials were evaluated involving 1,061 participants with fibromyalgia.

Results: This meta-analysis of studies found "that acupuncture alone or combined with cupping therapy was superior to conventional medications on reducing pain scores...... acupoint stimulation appears to be effective in treating fibromyalgia compared with medications." December 2013, *Evidence Based Complementary Alternative Medicine*.

✔ **Massage therapy**, to relax your muscles and joints to release some of your body's own natural painkillers.

✔ **Yoga and Tai Chi**, which have been found in some studies to be helpful in relieving fibromyalgia symptoms.

Other natural treatments include:

Herbal Supplement

✔ **Chlorella**: Several studies of chlorella supplementation have shown it to be effective in relieving the symptoms of fibromyalgia in some patients. May 2001, *Alternative Therapeutic Health Medicine*; and another study May 2000, *Phytotherapy Research*.

Natural Practices

✔ **Biofeedback:** To determine the effect of biofeedback exercises on pain from fibromyalgia, researchers did a meta-analysis of seven published studies involving 321 fibromyalgia patients.

Results: "In comparison to control groups, biofeedback significantly reduced pain intensity with a large effect size." September 2013, *Evidence Based Complementary Alternative Medicine.*

✔ **Cognitive Behavioral Therapy:** A group of girls aged 8 to 17 years were treated for symptoms of juvenile primary fibromyalgia using cognitive behavioral techniques (progressive muscle relaxation and guided imagery) to reduce pain and facilitate sleep.

Results: "In the majority of patients such techniques were effective in reducing pain and facilitating improved functioning." October 1992, *Journal of Rheumatology.*

✔ **Guided Imagery:** A group of 55 women with previously diagnosed fibromyalgia pain were divided into two groups. One received relaxation training and guided instruction in how to generate pleasant imagery in order to distract themselves from their pain. A control group received treatment as usual.

Results: Concluded the study authors: "Pleasant imagery was an effective intervention in reducing fibromyalgia pain during the 28-day study period." May 2002, *Journal of Psychiatric Research.*

✔ **Mindfulness:** Fifty-eight females with fibromyalgia were divided into a Mindfulness group, or a social support group in this Swiss study at the Department of Internal Medicine, University of Basel Hospital. During the eight-week program, both groups were monitored for three types of pain associated with fibromyalgia.

Result: The researchers concluded that mindfulness provided "significantly greater benefits than the control intervention," and a three-year follow-up of mindfulness group participants found "sustained benefits" for all three pain measures. 2007, *Psychotherapy Psychosomatics.*

✔ **Music therapy**: In France, scientists tested the effects of soothing music on 87 patients suffering from **lumbar pain, fibromyalgia, inflammatory disease or neurological disease.** These folks received at least two daily sessions of music and then when they returned home from the hospital, they continued this music intervention as part of their treatment.

Result: "This music intervention method appears to be useful in managing chronic pain as it enables a significant reduction in the consumption of medication." October 2011, *The Clinical Journal of Pain.*

✔ **Relaxation Response**: A review was conducted of the results from several hundred studies examining the relaxation response.

Results: It was found that headaches and insomnia were two of the more effective treatments that the technique can be used for. 2001, *Journal of Alternative and Complementary Medicine.*

✔ **Exercise**: Those who suffer from fibromyalgia often become afraid of exercise fearing it will make their pain worse. That sets in motion a vicious cycle. The lack of exercise actually worsens conditions in fibromyalgia. In 2007, Daniel Rooks, a Ph.D. assistant professor of medicine at Harvard Medical School, led a research team which published research showing that engaging in strength training, vigorous walking, and even just stretching exercises acts as a catalyst to reduce physical pain in fibromyalgia patients. Exercise is categorized as a 'good' pain because it helps to release endorphins, your own natural painkillers. For best results, Professor Rooks and other experts have recommended that fibromyalgia patients form their own exercise groups so this support group can help them to maintain an exercise routine.

✔ **Far-Infrared Sauna**: Japanese scientists recruited 44 female fibromyalgia patients and put them through a 12-week thermal therapy (far-infrared sauna) once a day combined with underwater exercise once a day.

Results: "All of the patients reported significant reductions in pain and symptoms of up to 77% after the 12-week thermal therapy program, which remained relatively stable during the 6-month follow-up period." August 2011, *Complementary Therapy Clinical Practice*.

✔ **Medical Marijuana**: An overview of numerous randomized controlled trials examining the use of cannabinoids (a marijuana compound) in treating fibromyalgia concluded that cannabinoids offer "preliminary evidence of efficacy" as a pain treatment approach. November 2011, *British Journal of Clinical Pharmacology*.

✔ **Yoga**: Canadian scientists testing how to reduce symptoms of chronic pain in women with fibromyalgia had the study participants do a program of 75 minutes of hatha yoga twice weekly over a period of eight weeks.

Results: Practicing yoga reduced the symptoms of chronic pain in the women. It was the first study to evaluate the effect of yoga on elevating cortisol levels in the body, which seems to be the natural chemical mechanism by which pain is reduced following a yoga workout. July 2011, *Journal of Pain Research*.

Gout

If you are over the age of 40—though it can happen sooner— you may wake up in the middle of the night feeling a sudden pain and burning sensation in the joint of your big toe. It can happen in other parts of your body, but the big toe is the most common area for gout to get its pain tendrils into you.

It will feel as if your big toe has been set on fire from the inside. Even the weight of a thin sheet pressing on your toe can make the pain feel unbearable. It mostly happens to men, maybe because men are such big beer drinkers. Women raise their risk of getting gout after menopause. It can occur not just in the big toe joint, but in your wrists, hands, ankles, and knees. The reason for it is a high level of uric acid in your blood which can trigger the episode of gout by forming urate crystals in your joints.

Too much alcohol can cause it (all kinds of alcohol, but particularly beer and fatty foods); so can some prescription medications for high blood pressure trigger it. If you have one episode, you are likely to have another, though it could take years for that to happen.

There are lifestyle changes necessary to lessen the pain and other symptoms of gout. Endorsed by Mayo Clinic, these changes include:

- ✔ **Drinking water**: You will need to drink up to four liters of pure water a day to help flush out the uric acid in your system.

- ✔ **Limit meat intake**: This means cutting down or eliminating the amount of meat, fish, and poultry that you consume since these meats contribute to your production of uric acid.

- ✔ **Avoid alcohol**: During an attack of gout avoid consuming any alcohol in any form. Alcohol will contribute to prolonging and intensifying your symptoms.

Herbs, Foods, and Supplements

- ✔ **Cherries (tart)**: Try eating **cherries and drinking cherry juice**, which are known to lower uric acid levels in the body. Researchers at Tufts University produced evidence that people who suffer from gout had a 50% lower risk of more gout attacks if they ate an average of one cup of cherries, about 20 in all, on a daily basis. If they took a cherry extract, they still reduced by 40% their risk of more gout attacks. This was a significant indicator that tart cherries fight gout pain. In some patients with gout, the cherries took away the gout symptoms and gout attacks for the rest of their life.

- ✔ **Blueberries, blackberries and raspberries** may also help. Drink large amounts of **pure water** along with the berries.

- ✔ **Fruits such as oranges** can help to lower uric acids levels, so consume them in large quantities while having a gout attack.

- ✔ **Coffee** consumption may also contribute to reducing uric acid levels in some people, so experiment and see if that works for you.

- ✔ **Breathing and relaxation exercises and meditation** may all be beneficial in helping you to deal with the pain until the gout attack subsides.

Headaches

There are several different types of headaches with a variety of possible causes. Stress can be a trigger. Muscle tension in your neck and shoulders can bring on a headache. Too much alcohol consumed the night before is another cause. Feeling depressed can bring on a headache. An allergic response to food can sometimes be blamed, such as what many people experience when they consume MSG, a flavor enhancer, in a Chinese restaurant.

Don't forget that dehydration can cause headaches, so drink a large glass of pure water if you feel a headache coming on, just in case it's due to not having consumed enough water during the day. Also keep in mind that caffeine can cause a headache if you consume too much, and can cause headaches as you withdraw from a caffeine dependency.

The worst category of headache by far, of course, is the migraine which, when it strikes suddenly, makes you feel like your head is about to split open. (You will find more on natural remedies for migraines later in this list of maladies.)

- ✔ **Feet soaking.** This is an old folk remedy but many people swear it works. Soak your feet in hot water when you feel a headache. Apparently, by drawing blood down to your feet, you relieve the pressure that built up on the blood vessels in your head and that turns down the pain volume. You can even add hot mustard powder to the water if your headache is bad enough. That is supposed to work wonders. Finally, add in a cold compress on your forehead either during or immediately after your hot foot soak. Since the effect of cold is to constrict the blood vessels in your head, this vessel shrinkage may stop them from pressing on nerves that are often a cause of headaches.

- ✔ **Head and thumb massage.** You can do this on your own, though it might be helpful to have someone else do the manipulations, especially if the headache is debilitating. First, you can try massaging the web of skin that you see between the base of your thumb and forefinger, using a firm circular motion, and then switch to the other hand. Try this for a few minutes. This form of acupressure sometimes works. If not, place your thumbs on either side of your head, at your temples, and press hard, then move your thumbs in a circular motion for several minutes. See if that relieves the pressure and pain intensity. You may need to repeat this process several times, even alternating between massaging the web of your thumb skin and massaging your temples.

✔ **Biofeedback**: Ten children with chronic headaches attending an outpatient pediatric neurology clinic practiced relaxation with biofeedback and "learned to associate successful relaxation with positive pain-free virtual images of themselves."

Results: "Ratings of pain, daily functioning, and quality of life improved significantly at 1 and 3 months post-treatment." May 2013, *Pain Medicine*.

✔ **Guided Imagery**: To gauge the effects of a guided imagery practice on chronic tension-type headaches, 129 patients with chronic tension-type headaches were recruited to listen daily to a guided imagery audiocassette tape for a month. Another 131 patients with the same condition were given individual attention but no guided imagery. This was the control group.

Results: Those in the guided imagery group reported by three to one over the control group a "much better" improvement in headache frequency, headache severity, quality of life, and disability symptoms caused by headaches. Concluded the team of researchers: "Guided imagery is an effective adjunct therapy for the management of chronic tension-type headache." May 1999, *Headache, The Journal of Head and Face Pain*.

✔ **Relaxation Response**: A review was conducted of the results from several hundred studies examining the relaxation response.

Results: It was found that headaches and insomnia were two of the more effective treatments for which the technique can be used. 2001, *Journal of Alternative and Complementary Medicine*.

Some Herbal Remedies to Try

✔ **Bay Leaves**: There are compounds called parthenolides in bay leaves which James A. Duke's research indicates may inhibit the release of serotonin from platelet blood cells in your head. It is this platelet release which may be a trigger for migraine headaches.

✔ **Feverfew**: This herb has reportedly helped a lot of people suffering from migraine headaches. Dr. Duke said he would use it in combination with bay leaves if he suffered from a migraine. "Feverfew works for about two-thirds of those who use it consistently," noted Duke. You can eat the feverfew leaves, but you can also use two to eight leaves to make a tea. Don't boil the leaves, just add them to boiled water and let them leach their parthenolides into the water. (Pregnant women are urged not to take feverfew due to a possibility of miscarriage.)

In a June 2009 study appearing in the *Clinical Journal of Pain*, scientists reviewed all of the medical literature on studies that examined links between migraine headaches and food triggers, vitamins and supplements. Some of the food and food additive triggers identified were: aspartame, monosodium glutamate (MSG), nitrates, nitrites, tyramine, phenylethylamine.

Concluded the study review: "We recommend the use of the following supplements in the preventative treatment of migraines, in decreasing order of preference: **magnesium, Petasites hybridus, feverfew, coenzyme Q10, riboflavin, and alpha lipoic acid**."

✔ **Evening Primrose**: Containing a pain relieving compound called phenylalanine, herbalists recommend that evening primrose oil be taken daily, six to eight capsules at a time. Other good sources of phenylalanine are sunflower seeds, watercress, bean sprouts, soybeans, swamp cabbage, peanuts, and lentils.

✔ **Fresh or Powdered Ginger**: This is a traditional remedy some people find effective because it contains anti-inflammatory agents. You can drink it by grinding up a half-teaspoon and stirring it into a glass of water. Some research done in Denmark has shown that fresh or powdered ginger consumption helps prevent a migraine by blocking prostaglandins, hormone-like substances, but you need to know yourself well enough to sense the onset symptoms of a migraine to take the ginger.

✔ **Lavender Essential Oil**: If you gently massage drops of lavender essential oil on your temples and forehead, you might find the aroma to be a relaxant which will help to ease the severity of a headache or migraine. You can also use peppermint oil and its soothing menthol in the same fashion, or mix the two oils.

✔ **Homeopathy**: Practitioners of homeopathy recommend remedies based on the possible cause of the headache. For instance, if you drank too much alcohol, a homeopath might suggest taking something called **pulsatilla**, or if the headache pain is more emotional then **gelsemium** or **ignatia** might be the recommendation. Sun related headaches would be treated with **belladonna**, whereas a headache from a fall or injury might get an **arnica** suggestion.

Technology Might Help

✔ **Electromagnetic Stimulation**: If all else fails in your natural remedy toolbox, you might try a device which sends low-level electromagnetic waves to adjust your own brain waves so you have less sensitivity to the pain. Under the brand names Empulse and Trimed, the devices are about the size of a large watch. It must be individually programmed for you using a computerized brain frequency analyzer before it can be effective.

Joint Pain

You don't need to have full-blown arthritic conditions to experience joint pain.

Whether the pain in your joints is located in your ankles, feet or legs, if it's not from an injury or from an arthritic condition, it's often due to problems in your muscular/skeletal system or poor circulation. This was probably intensified by carrying around too many pounds and not observing a healthy posture, particularly when sitting.

It should be needless to say if you have a joint dislocation, or if you can't move the affected joint, or numbness has set in, you should be seeing a mainstream medical practitioner. Beyond that, if you are suffering from a joint sprain or strain, natural alternative remedies may be helpful for you.

Much as with muscle pain, some symptoms for sprains and strains are the same—pain and swelling. But with sprains there is usually some bruising. When it comes to strains, there is the acute resulting from injury, and chronic strain brought about by any repetitive movement, such as swinging a tennis racket.

✔ **Rest, Ice, Compression, and Elevation**

You will find information about R.I.C.E., as Mayo Clinic calls it, under the section on muscle pain treatments. The key result you want from these four steps is to reduce swelling. The more swelling you have in the joint, the more pain you can probably expect.

✔ **Cold Compress**

Alternate between a cold compress using ice wrapped in cloth applied to the painful joint, then later follow it up with a hot Epsom salts bath where you soak for longer than a normal bath.

✔ **Massage**

That should be a no-brainer. A gentle massage of the painful area can help to reduce inflammation. You can also add some essential oils to the massage oil—peppermint, lavender, and chamomile are good choices.

✔ **Drink Lots of Water**

That doesn't mean alcoholic or caffeinated drinks. It means lots of pure drinking water to flush out your system.

Herbs and Supplements

✔ **Herbs**: The herbal combination of **scutellaria and acacia** may be helpful for treating joint pain, according to nutritional biochemist Shawn M. Talbott.

✔ **Glucosamine Sulfate**: There is persuasive research evidence that glucosamine supplements can relieve **joint pain**, particularly offering relief for **osteoarthritis pain** in the knee, according to Dr. David C. Leopold, director of Integrative Medical education at the Scripps Center for Integrative Medicine in San Diego. Glucosamine is often combined with chondroitin to intensify its pain relieving effects, so be sure to look for a supplement with these ingredients.

Migraines

Similar to normal headaches but much more intense—if you've ever had one, you know exactly what I mean—migraines have been likened to brain surgery without anesthesia being done from the inside out.

The intense throbbing sensation of a migraine is sometimes accompanied by nausea, vomiting, sensitivity to sound and bright lights, and even a visual disturbance effect called an aura stimulated by your nervous system. That is one reason why migraine sufferers often try to isolate themselves by lying down in dark quiet rooms in an attempt to ride out the symptoms. Migraines can last for hours or even days. This condition often shows up in childhood. If either of your parents suffered from migraines, you are more likely to experience them, too.

What feels like a migraine could also be a more serious health problem. Physicians warn that you should go to an emergency room or seek a physician immediately if the headache comes over you suddenly like a thunderclap, or if the headache comes with a fever, stiff neck, double vision, seizures or mental confusion. If you are beyond the age of 50 and have never suffered headaches before, the onset of a severe one could be a symptom of a more serious condition.

For prevention of migraines, exercise is important to stimulate blood flow to all parts of your body, particularly your brain. Certain odors or foods can be triggers and keeping a migraine diary can clue you in over time what may be causing the onset of migraines. Some women experience estrogen as being a trigger when it shows up in medications. Finally, getting too little or even too much sleep can contribute to the migraine occurrence, another reason why I have included an entire section on natural sleep aids for you later in this book.

It is said that migraines are another one of those medical conditions which can't be cured but can be managed. The same holds true for the pain associated with this condition. If you want to avoid prescription drugs as much as possible, there are lifestyle changes you can make to go along with the natural herbs and natural techniques which studies have found to be effective.

- ✔ **Muscle Relaxation Exercises**: Whether it is progressive muscle relaxation, doing yoga, or engaging in a meditation practice, learning to relax yourself on command can help to blunt the impact of stress triggers for the onset of a migraine, or ease the pain symptoms once a migraine begins. Mayo Clinic recommends trying all of these approaches.

  Other natural techniques for migraine suggested by Mayo Clinic specialists include: **acupuncture, biofeedback, massage therapy, and cognitive behavioral therapy**. Also suggested: **feverfew, high doses of riboflavin (vitamin B2), coenzyme Q10, and magnesium supplements.**

- ✔ **Acupressure or Reflexology**: Manipulating the pressure points on the web of skin between your thumb and first finger, and on your big toes (pressure on the sides, bottom, and top of both big toes) can relieve some of the head pain and pressure, just as with headaches.

  A total of 218 patients with persistent migraine headaches were involved in this study to test the effects of acupuncture applied in one session over 24 hours. One group was given real acupuncture treatment while a second group was administered 'sham' (fake) acupuncture.

  Results: Real acupuncture was effective whereas sham acupuncture was not. "Acupuncture is clearly effective in relieving pain and preventing migraine relapse or aggravation," concluded the study authors. June 2009, *Headache.*

- ✔ **Chiropractic Treatment**: Twenty-two studies involving 2,628 patients aged 12 to 78 years were compared and assessed for which non-invasive treatments work best for chronic headaches.

Results: For the treatment of migraine headache "there is evidence that spinal manipulation may be an effective treatment option." July 2004, *Cochrane Library.*

✔ **Craniosacral Therapy**: Developed by an osteopathic physician, this approach involves the gentle massage of bones in the skull to release tension. Though scientific evidence for its usefulness is sparse, a February 2013 study in *Complementary Therapies in Clinical Practice* did find some possible use in treating chronic migraine headaches.

✔ **Orgasms**: So at first blush this may sound like an oxymoron—having an orgasm while you are experiencing excruciating migraine headache pain. But there is scientific evidence that if you can distract yourself from the pain long enough to have sex culminating in an orgasm, the rush of endorphins from your climax may numb the migraine pain long enough for the pain cycle to be broken.

In one study, a survey was done with 800 migraine sufferers and another 200 persons who had chronic cluster headaches (one-sided recurring head pains) to assess their experience with sexual activity during headache attacks and whether sex and orgasm affected the intensity of the pain they felt.

Results: About one-third of the migraine patients experimented with having sex during a migraine or cluster headache and of those, 60% reported that they felt a moderate or complete reduction in pain. A few people reported that sex worsened their headaches, but they were a distinct minority. Even masturbation to orgasm may be helpful during a migraine attack. "Having an orgasm in any way, shape or form will help," said Alexander Mauskop, a neurologist and director of the New York Headache Center, in an interview with *LiveScience.* March 2013, *Cephalalgia.*

✔ **Relaxation Response**: Eighteen children between the ages of 8 and 12 were studied for the effect that relaxation response training would have on their migraine headaches over 15 weeks.

Results: The treatment group "experienced a significant reduction in headache symptoms" and this reduction in headache symptoms was maintained one year after treatment ended. April 1986, *Developments Medical Child Neurology.*

Foods, Herbs, and Essential Oils

✔ **Garlic and Onion**: Eating lots of garlic and onions are good for lots of cardiovascular ailments, and since the platelet cells in your blood are also involved in blood clotting and triggering migraines, it certainly wouldn't hurt for you to make those platelets less active by absorbing the blood thinner veggies garlic and onions.

✔ **Bay Leaves**: There are compounds called parthenolides in bay leaves which James A. Duke's research indicates may inhibit the release of serotonin from platelet blood cells in your head. It is this platelet release which may be a trigger for migraine headaches.

✔ **Feverfew**: This herb has reportedly helped a lot of people suffering from migraine headaches. Dr. Duke said he would use it in combination with bay leaves if he suffered from a migraine. "Feverfew works for about two-thirds of those who use it consistently," noted Duke. You can eat the feverfew leaves, but you can also use two to eight leaves to make a tea. Don't boil the leaves, just add them to boiled water and let them leach their parthenolides into the water. (Pregnant women are urged not to take feverfew due to a possibility of miscarriage.)

In a June 2009 study appearing in the *Clinical Journal of Pain*, scientists reviewed all of the medical literature on studies that examined links between migraine headaches and food triggers, vitamins and supplements. Some of the food and food additive triggers identified were: aspartame, monosodium glutamate (MSG), nitrates, nitrites, tyramine, phenylethylamine.

Concluded the study review: "We recommend the use of the following supplements in the preventative treatment of migraines, in decreasing order of preference: **magnesium, Petasites hybridus, feverfew, coenzyme Q10, riboflavin, and alpha lipoic acid.**"

✔ **Fresh or Powdered Ginger**: This is a traditional remedy some people find effective because it contains anti-inflammatory agents. You can drink it by grinding up a half-teaspoon and stirring it into a glass of water. Some research done in Denmark has shown that fresh or powdered ginger consumption helps prevent a migraine by blocking prostaglandins, hormone-like substances, but you need to know yourself well enough to sense the onset symptoms of a migraine to take the ginger.

✔ **Lavender Essential Oil**: If you gently massage drops of lavender essential oil on your temples and forehead, you might find the aroma to be a relaxant which will help to ease the severity of a headache or migraine. You can also use peppermint oil and its soothing menthol in the same fashion, or mix the two oils.

Technology Might Help

> ✔ **Electromagnetic Stimulation**: If all else fails in your natural remedy toolbox, you might try a device which sends low-level electromagnetic waves to adjust your own brain waves so you have less sensitivity to the pain. Under the brand names Empulse and Trimed, the devices are about the size of a large watch. It must be individually programmed for you using a computerized brain frequency analyzer before it can be effective.

Muscle pain

By way of definition, a sprain is stretching or tearing a ligament connecting one of your bones to one of your joints (it often feels like the muscle is involved), whereas a muscle strain is the stretching or tearing of a muscle or tendon, which is the fibrous tissue connecting your muscles to your bones.

Sprains are most common in the ankles, whereas strains usually show up in your hamstring muscles (back of your thighs) and in the muscles of your lower back. In the midst of pain you may not be able to distinguish between a sprain and a strain, though if you focus on the nature of the pain and its location you can begin to sort one type from another.

Both sprains and strains involve pain and swelling. But a sprain usually has bruising visible, whereas a strain will often have muscle spasms involved. You might also hear a popping sound in your joint when a sprain occurs. You will usually experience limited ability to move either the painful joint or the painful muscle. If you can't move or you feel numbness, it's advisable to see a doctor.

Home and Lifestyle Remedies

- ✔ **Rest, Ice, Compression, and Elevation**: This old home remedy for sprains and strains is really about applying common sense to your pain situation.

  - **Rest**. Experts advise that you try to avoid any activities that cause more pain or swelling, but don't avoid all physical activity because it's important to keep your mobility as much as possible. If it hurts you to place your weight on a sprained ankle, you can still peddle on an exercise bicycle using one leg and rest your injured ankle on a footrest.

  - **Ice**. You probably know this one. Place an ice pack on the injury as soon as possible. You should keep the injured area iced for up to 20 minutes. Repeat this several times a day for the first few days. Cold reduces your pain and swelling. If the area turns white, stop treatment immediately.

  - **Compression**. Compress the injured area with an elastic bandage to help keep down the swelling, but be sure you don't wrap the bandage too tightly. You should loosen the wrap if your pain increases or if the area becomes numb. Also loosen the wrap if swelling is occurring outside the wrapped area.

  - **Elevation**. Elevate the injured area above the level of your heart to help reduce the swelling and with it, the pain. This should especially be done at night. We all know how gravity can help to reduce swelling by draining excess fluid.

- ✔ **Massage**: Who doesn't like massages? Few people have an aversion to this sort of therapy. A gentle massage to the painful area and the skin around the soreness will help to stimulate blood flow. Combine the massage you get from someone, or the one you give yourself, with the essential oils treatment. Best of all worlds—soak in warm water with Epsom salts first, and then get a massage with an essential oils rub.

✔ **Use Epsom Salt**: A cup or two of Epsom salt dissolved in warm water will help your painful aching muscles. Soak the injured area for up to 15 minutes at a time. Magnesium sulfate is the main ingredient in Epsom salt and physical therapists know that magnesium is a natural muscle relaxant that also helps to reduce swelling.

✔ **Oral Magnesium**: Foods naturally high in magnesium include spinach, Swiss chard, squash, pumpkin seeds, black beans, flax seeds, cashews, and almonds.

✔ **Apple Cider Vinegar**: Anecdotal accounts portray apple cider vinegar as useful in dealing with muscle strains and sprains. You can mix a tablespoon of it in a glass of water and drink it, or you can directly rub it into the soreness or painful area.

✔ **Essential Oils**: Herbalists tout several different essential oils and blends of essential oils to help relieve muscle pain. Among them: peppermint with lemongrass; marjoram; and Roman chamomile. Add a drop or two of the essential oil to a tablespoon of olive oil or coconut oil and gently rub into the painful or sore area.

✔ **Herbs**: In his book *Natural Solutions for Pain-Free Living*, the nutritional biochemist Shawn M. Talbott, Ph.D., recommended several herbal remedies that his research indicates may be helpful. For muscle and soft tissue pain, you can try the anti-inflammatory herbal extracts **boswellia, ginger, turmeric, avocado/soy extracts, and scutellaria.**

✔ **Ginger**: For several thousand years, ginger has been used as a medicinal herb. A study conducted at the University of Georgia on muscle pain and ginger supplements used 74 people divided into two groups. One group took a placebo (a sugar pill) while the second group took daily capsules containing two grams of ginger. A week later the two groups were asked to perform intense exercises designed to produce painful inflamed muscles. Based on a pain index, the ginger group had 24% less pain. The reason seemed to be that ginger inhibits the COX-1 and COX-2 enzymes that produce inflammation causing compounds in your body. A daily 2-gram ginger supplement might do the trick to help prevent muscle pain (such as before an athletic event) or to treat the muscle pain once it begins, in which case 3 to 4 grams may be more advisable to take.

Results, an overview from the study authors: "This study demonstrates that daily consumption of raw and heat-treated ginger resulted in moderate-to-large reductions in muscle pain…our findings agree with those showing hypoalgesic effects of ginger in osteoarthritis patients and further demonstrate ginger's effectiveness as a pain reliever." September 2010, *Journal of Pain*.

Neck Pain

The longer you sit in front of a computer, peer over a steering wheel on a long drive, or do any other repetitive task that requires you to hold your head on your neck in a certain position for long periods of time, the more likely you are to develop pain in your neck. Poor posture is a key contributor.

If your neck pain comes with numbness, or loss of strength in your hands and arms, you need to seek medical attention because you may have a serious health condition. Otherwise, some of the natural remedies may be helpful to you in relieving this pain in your neck 'help me I can't get rid of this' feeling.

There are a variety of self-help techniques for you to try.

- ✔ **Heat and Cold Compression**: Just as with muscle or joint pain, if you apply an ice pack several times a day and follow that later with a heating pad, you can test what works best to reduce the inflammation and with it, the pain.

- ✔ **Acupressure**: Using your thumb or your fingertips, try putting steady pressure on the pain area. Keep the pressure on for three minutes or so. It's the same principle as when you apply pressure to a headache.

- ✔ **Acupuncture**: Studies have been mixed on its usefulness for neck pain, but it may be worth trying if your condition is chronic.

  To determine how effective acupuncture has been in clinical trials for neck pain, one of the three most frequently reported complaints of the musculoskeletal system, a team of seven scientists examined the results from 10 studies that used acupuncture treatments for chronic neck pain.

  Results: "There is moderate evidence that acupuncture relieves pain…and moderate evidence that acupuncture is more effective than inactive treatments for relieving pain post-treatment and this is maintained at short-term follow-up." July 2006, *Cochrane Database System Review*.

- ✔ **Biofeedback**: Thirty secondary school teachers aged 25 to 45 years with neck pain received training in pressure biofeedback; a control group got conventional exercise therapy only. Pain measurements were taken before the study and after two and four weeks of training.

Results: More improvement in pain and disability was experienced by the biofeedback group. June 2013, *Journal Physical Therapy Science.*

✔ **Chiropractic Manipulation**: This is different from massage because the chiropractic adjustment is intended to realign your spine to better support your neck. Any misalignment could be the source of your neck pain.

Researchers gathered together the results from 27 study trials conducted assessing whether neck manipulation, such as that performed by chiropractors, lessened pain.

Results: "Moderate quality evidence" showed that cervical manipulation lessened pain in neck pain patients. August 2010, *Manual Therapy.*

✔ **Capsaicin Rub**: This compound derived from hot peppers has found its way into numerous natural drug store products promising pain relief. Some research has shown chronic neck pain improvement if capsaicin cream is used at least four times a day over a month or more.

Once again, as with other pain related maladies, try using capsaicin cream with acupressure, massage, and some of the other natural remedies to get the maximum benefit of a synergy which can occur between all of the approaches. Synergies are much more powerful than any one technique used on its own.

✔ **Massage**: It's certainly worth trying a gentle massage focusing on your neck if it's done by a licensed practitioner.

✔ **Sarno's Mind/Body Prescription**: See the section under Back Pain for information about how a treatable psychosomatic illness may be the root cause of your neck pain symptoms.

Nerve Pain (peripheral neuropathy)

Nerve damage can result in pain, numbness, and weakness in your hands or feet. The pain is often described as a burning sensation. The nerve damage can result from diabetes, infections, traumatic injury, alcoholism, autoimmune disease, or even environmental toxins. Repetitive physical stress related to your job can trigger it. Certain types of neuropathy are also inherited.

A range of nerve types in your body can be affected by the damage: autonomic nerves connected to blood pressure, heart rate, and digestion; motor nerves that affect how your body moves and your mobility; and your sensory nerves which affect heat, pain or touch sensations.

Lifestyle Changes Recommended

- ✔ **Regular Exercise**: This one keeps coming up in connection with all sorts of pain. Just walking three times a week may help to reduce your pain from a neuropathy condition. That's according to Mayo Clinic. **Yoga** and **Tai Chi** have also been documented to have benefits in managing such pain.

- ✔ **Quit Smoking**: You've heard this one before, too. Your circulation is affected by cigarette smoking, which constricts your blood vessels. That will make pain from neuropathy worse.

- ✔ **Massage**: Whether you have it done professionally or have a friend or partner do it, massage stimulates your circulation and your nerves, and that can't help but be beneficial in the pain department.

Techniques for Neuropathy Pain

- ✔ **Acupuncture**: You may need multiple treatments over time to see improvement, but this technique may reduce your pain symptoms.

Certain chemotherapies given during cancer treatment can cause peripheral neuropathy in cancer patients and this persistent pain impairs the patient's quality of life. In this study 18 cancer patients with neuropathy were given a course of six weekly acupuncture sessions.

Results: After the sessions, 82% of the patients reported an improvement in their pain levels and other symptoms. Some also reported a reduced need for pain medications and improved sleeping patterns. September 2011, *Acupuncture Medicine*.

✔ **Biofeedback**: Here is how Mayo Clinic described the process: "Biofeedback may help reduce your stress and cope with pain you may experience from peripheral neuropathy. During a biofeedback session, the therapist applies electrical sensors to different parts of your body to monitor your body's physiological response to your peripheral neuropathy symptoms. The biofeedback device then teaches you how your body responds using cues, such as a beeping sound or flashing lights. This feedback can help you associate your body's response with certain physical functions."

Herbs and Related Substances

✔ **Alpha-lipoic Acid**: Europeans have used this antioxidant as a peripheral neuropathy treatment for a long time. It may affect your blood sugar levels, but it may be worth a try if nothing else is working to subdue the pain.

✔ **Curcumin**: This Indian curry spice is a remedy for many maladies in the traditional medicine of India; for people who have peripheral neuropathy as a result of diabetes, taking curcumin supplements may be a good choice, advise some naturopathic doctors.

✔ **Fish Oil**: You can't discount those omega-3 fatty acids in fish oil as an inflammation fighter. This supplement may improve your blood flow enough for you to notice a reduction in the severity of pain.

Osteoarthritis

If you live long enough, you are destined to contract the debilitating joint condition called osteoarthritis, say medical specialists. It's the most common form of arthritis and it occurs most frequently in your knees. The more added pounds you gain later in life, the more you increase your chances of getting osteoarthritis.

Exercise is one of the best preventive strategies, along with losing those excess pounds. You need to strengthen the muscles around your joints. Water-based exercises may be the best because you place less stress on your joints, particularly in your knees.

Prescription drugs, cortisone shots, lubrication injections, joint replacement surgery, that's most of the starting lineup of therapies used by mainstream medicine. At Mayo Clinic they do give patients the option of trying out natural pain reliever and pain reduction techniques. Here are some of them.

✔ **Hot and Cold**: This one comes up a lot for many varieties of pain. You alternate applications of heat and cold to relieve stiffness, reduce muscle spasms, and make the pain more bearable.

✔ **Acupuncture**: Even if you have an aversion to needles, try this technique and keep in mind beforehand that the needles are tiny and the pricking sensation is less intense than a vaccination shot. Some research indicates that acupuncture can relieve pain and improve mobility in some people with knee osteoarthritis.

In this study, 160 knee osteoarthritis patients were divided into two groups: a therapy group that tested acupuncture once a day combined with heat-sensitive moxibustion applied around knee joints, and a Western medication group using glucosamine sulfate capsules (two capsules three times a day) along with sodium hyaluronate and triamcinolone acetonide acetate injections.

Results: After five weeks of treatment "results in the combined therapy {acupuncture} group was superior remarkably to the Western medication group." At a six-month follow-up, the acupuncture patients still had less pain and better knee function than the Western medicine group. There also were many fewer adverse reactions in the acupuncture group." September 2011, *Acupuncture Medicine.*

✔ **Glucosamine and Chondroitin**: Mayo Clinic specialists claim the verdict isn't completely in on the usefulness of these nutritional supplements, but some people with osteoarthritis swear by them as pain relievers. So maybe it's worth trying. Physicians warn, however, that you shouldn't take them if you use blood thinners.

There is persuasive research evidence that glucosamine supplements can relieve joint pain, particularly offering relief for osteoarthritis pain in the knee, according to Dr. David C. Leopold, director of Integrative Medical education at the Scripps Center for Integrative Medicine in San Diego. Glucosamine is often combined with chondroitin to intensify its pain relieving effects, so be sure to look for a supplement with these ingredients.

✔ **Vitamin C**: A group of 640 persons were evaluated for osteoarthritis of the knee in this study. Those who consumed the most vitamin C (which was an average of 500 mg a day) "had a reduced risk of developing knee pain" and for those who already had knee pain, the vitamin supplement lessened the severity of their pain and slowed the progression of the disease." April 1996, *Arthritis & Rheumatism.*

Try Some Mind-Body Practices

Writing in a May 2007 issue of the journal *Pain Medicine*, researchers did a systematic review of studies done on eight types of mind-body interventions for adults with chronic pain. The mind-body therapies examined were biofeedback, progressive muscle relaxation, meditation, guided imagery, hypnosis, Tai Chi, Qigong, and yoga. Altogether, 20 trials of these techniques were included in the analysis, most done on study participants 50 years and older.

Result: Support was found "for the efficacy of progressive muscle relaxation plus guided imagery for osteoarthritis pain." Some support was found "for **meditation and Tai Chi** for improving function or coping in older adults with low back pain or osteoarthritis." As for **biofeedback**, "both older and younger adults had significant reductions in pain following the intervention." Furthermore, "**Tai Chi, yoga, hypnosis and progressive muscle relaxation** were significantly associated with pain reduction."

✔ **Biofeedback and Yoga**: A total of 30 persons with knee osteoarthritis were divided into two experimental groups. Group A received EMG biofeedback, knee muscle strengthening exercises, and did Iyengar yoga for eight weeks. Group B did the EMG feedback and exercises without yoga.

Results: "Patients in both groups experienced significant reduction in pain and improvements in functional ability… adding Iyengar yoga along with conventional therapy provides better results in chronic unilateral knee osteoarthritis in terms of pain and functional disability." July 2013, *International Journal of Yoga.*

✔ **More Iyengar Yoga**: A team of scientists in Texas evaluated studies which had been done on Qigong, Tai Chi, and yoga in treating pain and other symptoms associated with osteoarthritis.

Results: They found studies showing that Iyengar yoga, emphasizing strength, flexibility, and relaxation, is a practice that "has been shown to reduce pain" in osteoarthritis patients. July 2011, *Arthritis.*

Another study focused just on Iyengar yoga and had volunteers over the age of 50, all with knee osteoarthritis, do 90-minute classes once a week for eight weeks.

Results: "Statistically significant reductions in pain" were observed and no adverse effects occurred as a result of doing the yoga." August 2005, *Journal of Alternative and Complementary Medicine.*

✔ **Guided Imagery**: A group of 28 women with diagnosed osteoarthritis were randomly assigned to a control group or a treatment group. The treatment consisted of listening twice a day to a 10- to-15-minute audio-taped script. This script guided the women in progressive muscle relaxation.

Result: Compared to the control group, who reported no differences in their pain levels, those women in the guided imagery group "reported a significant reduction in pain and mobility difficulties at week 12." 2004, *Pain Management Nursing.*

Six years later (March 2010) another study in *Pain Management Nursing* described how 30 older adults with osteoarthritis went through a four-month trial of guided imagery with relaxation. Not only did the technique reduce their pain symptoms, they were able to significantly reduce their prescribed arthritis medications. This finding was important because it demonstrated that a natural mind-body technique could be as effective as pain drugs in some people.

✔ **Tai Chi**: A team of scientists in Texas evaluated studies which had been done on Qigong, Tai Chi, and yoga in treating pain and other symptoms associated with osteoarthritis.

Results: They found five randomized controlled trials which documented Tai Chi as "significantly reducing pain intensity in osteoarthritis patients." July 2011, *Arthritis.*

In a review of study evidence for Tai Chi in relieving pain for a variety of chronic pain conditions, the author focused on five pain conditions. Of these, three had supporting evidence.

Results: "Tai Chi seems to be an effective intervention in osteoarthritis, low back pain, and fibromyalgia." July 2012, *Anesthesia Pain Medicine.*

✔ **Qigong**: Scientists evaluated studies which had been done on Qigong, Tai Chi, and yoga in treating pain and other symptoms associated with osteoarthritis.

Results: They found "some studies in China reported improvement of severe arthritis symptoms" including a reduction in pain. July 2011, *Arthritis.*

Foods and Herbal Remedies

✔ **Ginger**: While the focus has often been on relieving muscle pain, this remedy has research backing it as a treatment for osteoarthritis. For several thousand years ginger has been used as a medicinal herb. A study conducted at the University of Georgia on muscle pain and ginger supplements used 74 people divided into two groups. One group took a placebo (a sugar pill) while the second group took daily capsules containing two grams of ginger. A week later the two groups were asked to perform intense exercises designed to produce painful inflamed muscles. Based on a pain index, the ginger group had 24% less pain. The reason seemed to be that ginger inhibits the COX-1 and COX-2 enzymes that produce inflammation-causing compounds in your body. A daily 2-gram ginger supplement might do the trick to help prevent muscle pain or to treat the muscle pain once it begins, in which case 3 to 4 grams may be more advisable to take.

The authors of this research observed: "This study demonstrates that daily consumption of raw and heat-treated ginger resulted in moderate-to-large reductions in muscle pain… our findings agree with those showing hypoalgesic effects of ginger in osteoarthritis patients and further demonstrate ginger's effectiveness as a pain reliever." September 2010, *Journal of Pain.*

✔ **Purple Passion Fruit Peel Extract**: You may be wondering 'what the heck is that?' It's a flavonoid-rich dietary supplement made from purple passion fruit. There is some research evidence that it helps reduce pain and stiffness in adults with **knee osteoarthritis**. In a study by a team of 11 nutrition scientists, they took 33 knee osteoarthritis patients and had them take 150 mg a day of purple passion fruit peel extract pills for two months. Another group with an equal number of patients (the control group) took a placebo (a sugar pill) instead of the supplement.

Results: After 60 days, reductions averaging nearly 20% were recorded for pain and stiffness severity among the supplement takers. Among the control group, all measures of pain and stiffness increased. "The results of this study show that {the supplement} substantially alleviated osteoarthritis symptoms. This beneficial effect may be due to its antioxidant and anti-inflammatory properties." September 2010, *Nutrition Research.*

✔ **Cherries (tart)**: At the Oregon Health & Science University, researchers studied tart cherries by evaluating its effects on 20 women suffering from painful osteoarthritis. Drinking tart cherry juice twice a day was found to be effective in reducing this type of arthritis pain. This May 2012 study noted how the active ingredients in tart cherries are anthocyanins, which have antioxidant and anti-inflammatory properties. The study authors observed that tart cherries can help relieve osteoarthritis pain without any side effects that are often associated with arthritis medications.

Premenstrual Syndrome (and menstrual pain)

For women still menstruating every month brings the same old litany of symptoms—body pain, headaches, bloating, mood swings—varying in severity from one woman to the next, but still a big hassle for all.

Quite a few natural remedies for premenstrual syndrome exist, though they aren't widely publicized, which might explain why you've never heard of many of them. PMS isn't a condition to be endured—its symptoms can be managed safely.

To reduce the severity of symptoms each month, a few common sense approaches are recommended. For one, get at least 30 minutes of aerobic-type exercise every day. That's considered important to lower the amounts of free-circulating estrogen in your circulatory system. Exercise will also help to enhance your mood and relieve some of the stress which magnifies PMS symptoms.

Herbs and Dietary Recommendations

✔ **More Water and Fiber**: Medical authorities advise drinking at least eight 8-ounce glasses of water a day, cutting down on salt intake in the week before your period, and consuming a lot of high-fiber foods to help eliminate excess estrogen in your body.

✔ **Calcium**: You may not be getting enough of it, and it could help reduce your pain and other PMS symptoms. That was the finding of a study of 78 women who were given three months of daily calcium supplementation of 1,000 mg of calcium carbonate—73% of the women reported less severe symptoms, including pain. May 1989, *Journal of General Internal Medicine.*

✔ **Essential Fatty Acids**: By eliminating meat and dairy products from your diet and living on primarily plant-based foods, study evidence shows your production of estrogen will go down and your PMS symptoms will be lessened as you absorb more omega-3 fatty acids. That's guidance from Dr. Neal Barnard, who has reviewed the medical literature. (He doesn't recommend eating salmon and other fish to get your omega-3s; he makes a case that the plant-derived oils are superior in every respect.)

✔ **Chasteberry**: The ancient Greeks and Romans found the small berries from the chaste tree to be effective in treating PMS several thousand years ago. In our day and age research has shown the berries help to bring about a shift in the estrogen-progesterone ratio. Dr. James A. Duke, in his book *The Green Pharmacy,* even describes a study in which chasteberry was found superior to vitamin B6 in dealing with the symptoms of PMS.

✔ **Chinese Angelica**: Long used as an herbal treatment for PMS in traditional Chinese medicine, it has achieved renewed respectability. Take two capsules twice a day for PMS symptoms.

✔ **Evening Primrose**: This is another herb that pops up repeatedly as a pain reliever. In the case of PMS, chewing the seeds is a centuries-old Native American tribal remedy and only now is medical science affirming with a stamp of approval its many benefits.

✔ **Acupuncture/Acupressure**: A group of 32 women were involved in this study testing the effects of acupressure on menstrual pain and distress. (Acupressure uses the same body position points as acupuncture.)

Results: Acupressure was found to "have value in alleviating menstrual pain and menstrual distress in a high-stress life." December 2013, *Evidence Based Complementary Alternative Medicine*.

✔ **Relaxation Response**: Over five months the effects of the relaxation response on 46 women and their premenstrual symptoms, including pain, was assessed.

Results: "We conclude that regular elicitation of the relaxation response is an effective treatment for physical and emotional premenstrual symptoms and is most effective in women with severe symptoms." Those with severe symptoms saw a 58% improvement. April 1990, *Obstetrics & Gynecology*.

Rheumatoid Arthritis

Joint deformity and bone erosion can result if this disorder isn't treated properly or in time. When this chronic inflammatory disorder (an autoimmune disease) affects the lining of the small joints in your hands and feet, your immune system is mistakenly attacking your own body tissues to cause it.

It usually affects women more than men and typically develops beyond 40 years of age. As with other types of arthritis, the joints become stiff and tender, but in addition there is fatigue and small bumps of tissue which form under the skin of the arms. Symptoms often spread over time from your fingers and toes to your hips and shoulders.

Both steroids and non-steroidal anti-inflammatory drugs are typically prescribed by mainstream physicians, as well as medications in attempts to strengthen the immune system. Surgery may also be prescribed to repair the damaged joints.

✔ Natural remedies identified by Mayo Clinic and other medical authorities to manage rheumatoid arthritis pain include:

1. **Regular gentle exercise** to strengthen muscles around the joints. This exercise can be swimming or water aerobics.

2. **Tai Chi** is a combination of deep breathing and stretching and this movement therapy has shown some promise in studies for reducing the pain associated with rheumatoid arthritis.

3. Alternating **heat and cold** to relax the affected body areas. Cold may be best for this disorder because it helps reduce muscle spasms as it numbs and relaxes the painful areas.

4. Reduce stress in your life (yes, as with most everything, too much stress worsens the condition) by using **hypnosis, guided imagery, deep breathing**, and other relaxation techniques shown in studies to be effective in controlling pain. (For more information about these techniques and practices see the list later in this book section.)

5. Seed oils of **evening primrose, black currant**, and **borage** contain fatty acids found to be helpful in reducing stiffness and pain.

6. **Fish oil supplements** may also be helpful in pain and stiffness reduction.

7. Adopt a **vegetarian or vegan diet**. A series of studies in such prominent medical journals as *The Lancet, Arthritis Rheumatism*, and *Clinical Rheumatism* have produced evidence that at least half of all rheumatoid arthritis patients studied showed significant reductions in their pain and other symptoms once they adopted a plant-based diet. Dietary choices involving meats, eggs, and dairy products are a trigger for the onset of this disorder, and these food sensitivities contribute to a worsening of symptoms.

8. **Glucosamine Sulfate Supplements**: This is a favorite of Dr. Jacob Teitelbaum, medical director of the Center for Effective CFS/Fibromyalgia Therapies in Maryland. He believes that taking 500 mg three times a day will help your body to build cartilage in order to repair damage done by rheumatoid arthritis.

9. **Ginger Combined with Turmeric**: This is a favorite of Dr. James A. Duke, the expert on healing herbs. The curcumin in turmeric is a compound similar to ginger, call it a close cousin. Taken together, especially combined with food such as curries, can be a spicy, tasty, and potentially useful dietary regimen to adopt in reducing pain, inflammation, and other symptoms of rheumatoid arthritis.

✔ **Far-Infrared Sauna**: A team of researchers treated 17 rheumatoid arthritis patients for a period of four weeks with eight infrared sauna treatments.

Results: "Infrared sauna was well tolerated, and no adverse effects were reported, no exacerbation of disease. Pain and

stiffness decreased clinically, and improvements were statistically significant. Fatigue also decreased." January 2009,
Clinical Rheumatology.

✔ **Medical Marijuana**: An overview of numerous randomized
controlled trials examining the use of cannabinoids (a marijuana compound) in treating rheumatoid arthritis concluded
that cannabinoids offer "preliminary evidence of efficacy" as
a pain treatment approach. November 2011, *British Journal
of Clinical Pharmacology.*

Sciatica

Your sciatic nerve running from your lower back down your but-
tocks into the outer back of your legs can be a source of intense pain
when the nerve fibers become inflamed. Often the cause, according
to Mayo Clinic, is a herniated disk or a bone spur on your spine. This
can cause inflammation, pain, and even numbness in the affected
area. Severe cases can result in your loss of bladder or bowel function.

Those who have experienced sciatic pain describe it as ranging
from a mild or dull ache to sharp burning sensations that feel a little
like electric shocks being administered. It is said that usually just
one side of your body is affected. Your age (your spine changes),
your weight (obesity stresses your spine), and your occupation (lots
of heavy lifting) can be risk factors in developing a sciatic condition,
along with having a sedentary lifestyle or a job that has you sitting
for long periods of time.

Self-care steps you can take and professional help you can seek
to help relieve symptoms include:

✔ **Cold and Hot Packs**: Start with a cold pack on the painful
area for 20 minutes or so a day, then after a few days use
a hot pack, which can be a heating pad or a heat lamp. If
pain persists, try alternating the hot and cold applications.

✔ **Stretching Exercises**: Be gentle with yourself, but don't lay around idle when you could be slowly stretching to relieve the compression in your sciatic nerve. Make this a daily routine.

✔ **Acupuncture**: Though the studies are mixed on its usefulness in relieving sciatic pain, it may be worth trying since people seem to react differently to the effects of acupuncture and you may be one of the fortunate ones.

✔ **Chiropractic Manipulation**: Spinal adjustments are what chiropractors specialize in, so it wouldn't hurt to try this form of manipulation to decrease your pain and improve mobility.

Here are some of the herbs, besides the better known ginger, willow, and wintergreen, to treat the pain, as recommended by James A. Duke, Ph.D., an herbal authority formerly with the U.S. Department of Agriculture testing lab.

✔ **Hayseed**: You've probably heard the old slang expression 'he's such a hayseed'; as it turns out, the seed heads of various grasses have been known for centuries as being a therapy for painful joints, muscles, and the lower back, where the sciatic nerve is located. A compound called coumarin is in hayseed. It's known as a blood flow booster when applied externally to the skin. It's best used as a bath application. Draw up a hot bath, add the seed to it, and soak for a while.

✔ **Stinging Nettle**: Can making your skin sting by slapping it with the sprigs of this prickly plant help you tolerate pain? Apparently so. The stinging sensation, in James A. Duke's estimation, "in effect fools the nervous system into disregarding deeper pain." But there are also chemicals in the stingers which may help to trigger your body's own natural anti-inflammatories into action as additional pain relievers.

✔ **Chinese Angelica**: Some physicians in China have been known to inject small amounts of this mild sedative and anti-inflammatory into acupuncture points corresponding to the lower back and the sciatic nerve. Dr. Duke doesn't advise injecting it, but does think it can be taken as a tea or tincture for pain.

✔ **Mustard**: If you already like spicy mustard this one pain remedy may appeal to you. When used as a plaster on the skin, it creates a soothing feeling of warmth that helps to distract your brain from the sciatic pain.

Shingles

This viral infection can give you a painful red rash characterized by a stripe of blisters on one side of your body, though some people with shingles never develop the rash. If you had the chickenpox as a kid, you stand a greater chance of this virus making a return appearance because it has been dormant inside you all those years. Your odds are about one in five of getting it, say medical authorities. It's said to be extremely painful when it returns as shingles and it usually appears in folks 50 years of age or older.

The reappearance of the shingles virus, much as with the herpes virus, can be a sign of stress in your life not being handled, or an indicator that your immune system is being depressed. (Stress is a factor in depressing your immune system.) Dr. Neal Barnard, for one, has urged that we boost our immune system using a heavy intake of lowfat vegetarian foods. A daily multivitamin can also help in strengthening your immune system.

While there is no cure for shingles, say medical experts, you can manage the symptoms, including the pain, to make life more bearable. You really will want to reduce the pain because shingles can persist for years. Mainstream medicine has its own regimen of drugs to attack shingles (there are even several vaccines developed to prevent it), but once it emerges you can also try some natural alternative treatments.

Self-care steps you can take:

✔ **Cool or Cold Exposure**: Try taking cool water baths frequently, along with cold water compresses applied to the rash or pain radiating areas.

Nature has some treatments for viral illness, including shingles, pointed out James A. Duke, Ph.D., the expert on herbal remedies.

✔ **Lemon Balm**: It's a member of the mint family and some researchers have found it to be useful in treating the herpes virus, which is similar to the virus that causes shingles. Dr. Varro Tyler, longtime pharmacy professor at Purdue University, has investigated lemon balm and its anti-viral properties. He proposed making a tea from several teaspoons of dried lemon balm leaf and applying it on a cotton pad to the pain area at least several times a day. Dr. Duke suggested adding a mint herb—peppermint, spearmint, oregano, rosemary—and even put some licorice in it. You can drink the tea and apply it to the body area where the rash is found and the pain radiates.

✔ **Red Pepper**: Capsaicin, that ingredient which gives red peppers their hot flavor punch, can short-circuit the pain signals from the nerves just under your skin. Rather than buying over-the-counter ointments that contain it, you can mix your own by adding powdered red pepper to any white skin lotion and applying that several times a day to the pain area. A 1993 study appearing in the *Journal of the American Medical Association* found capsaicin cream to be an effective pain desensitizer which does its work by depleting a nerve chemical which contributes to pain signals.

✔ **Licorice**: If he had shingles, Dr. Duke said he would drink licorice in a tea and also apply it to the skin of the pain area. He quoted other herbal researchers in his *The Green Pharmacy*, relating that they saw "people with shingles whose pain and inflammation cleared up within three days following application of a licorice ointment on painful areas."

✔ **Chinese Angelica**: Chinese traditional medicine practitioners are known to use this powdered root in their treatments of shingles, and reports have been positive. You can also try absorbing it by drinking it as a tea.

✔ **Lysine**: Some food and herb researchers have recommended taking two 500-mg supplement tablets of lysine, an amino acid, three or so times a day for the pain symptoms of shingles. Dr. Neal Barnard in his book *Foods That Fight Pain* noted how a survey of people using lysine for shingles discovered 10% found little or no benefit, while 90% experienced it to be effective in reducing symptoms.

Soybeans and watercress both contain a lot of lysine so both may be worth eating. Other foods that Duke and others point to as high in lysine include lentil sprouts, lentils, black bean sprouts, spinach, asparagus, Chinese cabbage, and fenugreek.

Natural Healing Practices

✔ **Acupuncture**: A total of 102 patients with severe pain from shingles (herpes zoster) were divided into two groups. One group received acupuncture treatment for four weeks while the second group got standard pharmacological treatments.

Results: The acupuncture group received as much pain relief as did the standard drug treatments, and acupuncture worked without any adverse side effects. "This controlled and randomize trial provides the first evidence of a potential role

of acupuncture for the treatment of acute herpetic pain."
June 2011, *BMC Complementary Alternative Medicine.*

✔ **Tai Chi**: A total of 112 older adults aged 59 to 86 were given
Tai Chi classes for 25 weeks to evaluate the effect on resting
and vaccine-stimulated levels of cell-mediated immunity to
varicella zoster virus (shingles).

Results: The Tai Chi group compared to a health education
control group boosted the effectiveness of a vaccine against
the shingles virus and "the Tai Chi group also showed significant improvements in score for bodily pain." April 2007,
Journal of American Geriatric Society.

Sore Throat Pain

While a sore throat is typically known as the first sign of coming
down with a cold, it can also be caused by bacteria (as in strep throat),
by a virus, or even by chemical irritants you encounter in the work-
place. Other possible causes include allergies and acid reflux disease.

Inflammation of your throat, that familiar scratchiness and
pain when you swallow, is often accompanied by swollen tonsils
(if you still have your tonsils), throat dryness, and perhaps swollen
glands in your jaw or neck.

If you or your child experiences difficulty breathing or such
difficulty with swallowing that drooling occurs, see a physician as
soon as possible.

Home and folk remedies for sore throat pain have been around
for generations. Some of these you will have heard of, while a few
may be new to you.

✔ **Gargle with Saltwater**: This is an old favorite. Just combine
one teaspoon of common salt to eight ounces of warm water,
stir it up, and gargle with it before spitting it out and starting

over. Do it as often as you need to. The salt helps to soothe the irritation in your throat.

✔ **Honey**: This is another tried and proven home remedy in use for generations, probably as far back as ancient Egypt. Honey will help to draw fluids out of inflamed tissue in your throat. Honey also has an antibacterial effect. Just add a few teaspoons of honey to an herbal tea or just hot water. You can also combine lemon juice with the honey in water for an even more soothing remedy.

Herbal Remedies

✔ **Slippery Elm**: This stuff will coat your throat and help with soreness. Try using it as one teaspoon of the inner bark in powdered form absorbed in several cups of boiled water. You can both drink it and gargle it.

✔ **Eucalyptus**: A common sore throat treatment in Europe, where mainstream medicine endorses its use, the tea made from the leaf of eucalyptus has a soothing effect when you drink it and the oil of eucalyptus can also be used as an anti-inflammatory.

✔ **Licorice**: Another ancient remedy, studies have documented its usefulness in sore throat treatment, wrote Dr. James A. Duke in *The Green Pharmacy*. To make it from scratch, take five to seven teaspoons of the licorice root pieces and place them in three cups of water, bring to a boil, then simmer until much of the water is gone. Drink it as you would an herbal tea.

✔ **Honeysuckle**: An ancient Chinese medicine herb, you can use honeysuckle flower extracts for their antibacterial activities in your throat; add it to hot lemon water and slowly drink it. You can even throw in some licorice.

✔ **Echinacea**: Use this herb for its antiviral and antibacterial potential. Try about 200 mg in capsule form. Swallow it three or four times a day for best results.

Sunburn Pain

Most of us who have spent any time in the sun are familiar with this one— your skin reddens, feels hot to the touch, and the burn pain can last for days. Get sunburned badly enough times, especially while in childhood, and you increase your risk not just for liver spots and wrinkled skin, but for contracting skin cancer.

If severe enough, your sunburn may also be characterized by blistering, swelling, and headaches accompanied by fever. You can burn any part of your body, including your scalp, your earlobes, and your lips. Those areas can be particularly painful once burned.

If you see any signs of infection, which might include pus oozing from the blister burns, you need to see a doctor right away. Otherwise, there are some natural remedies which may help you to ease the pain and discomfort.

✔ **Cold Water Soak**: Immerse the burnt painful area in cold (not icy) water or use a cold compress for 10 minutes or more as soon as you can. This may offer some immediate relief from the initial symptoms.

✔ **Green Tea Compress**: Brew up a pot of your favorite herbal green tea. Once it has cooled, drench cloth with it and compress it to the sunburned area. Green tea has healing agent ingredients that may reduce inflammation.

✔ **Apply Aloe Vera Lotion**: This lotion has a soothing effect on painful skin because it contains natural anti-inflammatories. You can buy this gel at either a health food store or some drugstores.

✔ **Drink fluids**: You want to prevent dehydration from worsening your condition, so drink plenty of pure water, not sodas or alcohol, just pure water.

✔ **Peppermint Oil**: Rub this oil gently into the painful area. It can have an antiseptic effect that might speed the healing process.

✔ **Potato or Cucumber Rubs**: This home remedy has been around for generations and involves applying sliced cucumber or potato to the burned area to soothe the skin and lessen the effects of swelling.

Tooth Pain

An inflamed nerve in your tooth can cause a throbbing, sometimes excruciating pain. Enamel on your tooth has eroded and that allows tiny pieces of food to infiltrate the center of the tooth, triggering inflammation. Gum disease can also cause pain that you may think is tooth related.

Dealing with tooth pain has been a human preoccupation throughout history. Written accounts describe the ancient Chinese using arsenic in attempts to ease tooth pain, whereas Russians gargled using a vodka and garlic mixture. Other cultures simply chiseled out the offending tooth hoping for relief.

White flour and white sugar are among the most notorious stimulants for tooth decay and with it, tooth pain. Once you have a toothache, you will want to avoid white flour and white sugar along with food products containing them like the plague because they will further irritate the nerve in your tooth.

Among the 'folk remedies' and 'home remedies' emerging through trial and error over the centuries were the following:

✔ **Ice Massage**: This remedy involves acupressure combined with cold. Take an ice cube and rub it on that webbed area of your hand located between your index finger and your thumb. In acupressure (which is related to acupuncture), this area of your hand corresponds to a pressure point that counteracts pain in the body. This is the same webbed area where pressure is applied to relieve headaches. You can also press ice inside a cloth to the outside of your cheek where the toothache is being experienced. Repeat this until the pain diminishes.

✔ **Salt Water Rinse**: Just as some people use warm saltwater to gargle with when they have a sore throat, you can try the same approach with a toothache. Swish the warm saltwater around in your mouth for a few minutes, careful not to swallow any of it. Spit it out and try another mouthful. Just as the salt granules dry out the inflammation in your throat, so can they enter your tooth and the surrounding gum area to reduce the inflammation that is causing your pain.

✔ **Hydrogen Peroxide**: You should be careful with this one. You don't want to swallow hydrogen peroxide and you don't want to use it for more than three days or it can burn your gums. Having said that, this recognized germ killer can reduce infection in your tooth or gums and that will help diminish the pain. Holistic dentists recommend that you swish a mouthful of it around and keep it in your mouth for a minute or so. Then spit it out and rinse your mouth with water.

✔ **Homeopathy**: Practitioners of homeopathy suggest dissolving a tablet of Arnica 30X under your tongue every 15 minutes or so. You may find that your pain increases when your tooth is exposed to either hot or cold drinks. To combat the effects of cold beverages, try dissolving a tablet of Plantago major. For hot beverage reactions, try a tablet of Chamomilla 30X.

- ✔ **Acupressure**: This technique can be particularly useful if the pain flares up and feels unbearable. Simply press the thumb of one hand into an area of your other hand (backside of hand) where your index finger and the base of your thumb meet. For at least two minutes keep the pressure on this area to help trigger the release of your body's own pain relief chemicals, the endorphins.

Plant Remedies for Toothache

- ✔ **Clove Oil**: After soaking a cotton ball in oil of cloves, place it on the offending tooth or gum area and bite down. Keep it in place as long as possible for maximum results. Recent research has found clove oil to have analgesic and anesthetic properties (it contains eugenol), so this particular old remedy now has some science behind its usefulness. Don't ingest it, though it is harmless if you do. You can get some of the same effects and benefits if you take whole cloves and let the leaves moisten in your mouth; then bite down gently letting the leaves and their oil engulf the area of pain.

- ✔ **Ginger and Red Pepper**: In his studies of herbal pain remedies used by ancient and tribal cultures, Dr. James A. Duke usually tried them out on himself when he had an ache or pain. One such remedy he recommended was to mix crushed ginger and red pepper (preferably cayenne pepper) with water into a paste and then put some of it onto a cotton ball and place that on the throbbing tooth. Hold it in as long as you can stand it. The two ingredients in this paste act as counterirritants and also contain salicylates, aspirin-like chemicals and known pain relievers.

✔ **Toothache Tree**: That's right, there is a tree whose bark and berries are known to offer pain relief from toothache, so it came to be known as the toothache tree. James A. Duke reported that he chewed on the twigs of this tree and found it to have anesthetic qualities. You can chew the bark of this tree or make a tea out of its berries. Some herb shops are known to sell it.

✔ **Willow Bark**: Because willow bark contains salicin, similar to aspirin, chewing a wad of it and then keeping it atop the affected tooth or gum area can help to relieve your pain. A tea can also be made from the willow bark.

✔ **Aloe and Echinacea**: Some people swear by this remedy which combines capsules of powdered echinacea and pure aloe gel. Echinacea is food for treating infection while aloe gel can reduce inflammation. You create a paste from two echinacea capsules with some of the aloe gel. Place a wad of this paste around the offending tooth. Let it dissolve and use it again as needed.

✔ **Myrrh Rinse**: With a tincture of myrrh create a rinse for your mouth; myrrh can help with your inflammation, particularly swollen gums. To create it, the recommended formula is to dissolve by simmering a teaspoon of powdered myrrh in two cups of water for about 30 minutes, and then rinse your mouth with some of it at least four or five times during the day.

Wrist Pain (carpal tunnel syndrome)

A pinched nerve in your wrist can lead to this progressively painful condition, radiating through your hand and wrist and up your arm. The most common cause is repetitive motion of your wrist in typing, piano playing, using vibrating tools, or performing some other duties, usually work related. Rheumatoid arthritis can also trigger it. So can diabetes.

Carpal tunnel is actually a narrow passage on the palm side of your wrist which protects the main nerve to your hand. Numbness and pain can result from the compression of this nerve. It can be a debilitating condition that sabotages your job, your sleep, and your peace of mind. Up to 10% of the U.S. population experiences this condition at some point in their life, according to the American Academy of Neurology. Usually mainstream medicine treats this condition with cortisone shots or surgery, which means more pain to endure.

There are ways to relieve carpal tunnel syndrome and the pain associated with it and you don't necessarily need surgery. Dr. Jacob Teitelbaum, a pain specialist, has noted how "in almost all of my patients, their carpal tunnel syndromes have resolved by simply using vitamin B6 (250 mg daily), Armour thyroid hormone, and a wrist splint for six weeks." This splint is designed to keep your hand in a neutral position in order to take stress off the nerve. You should wear it at night and also for as long as you can during the day.

Other natural pain relief approaches recommended by Dr. Teitelbaum include acupuncture, osteopathic manipulation, chiropractic manipulation, and myofascial release.

More Techniques for Relief

- ✔ **Ultrasound Therapy**: Specialists at Mayo Clinic recommend this approach. It involves high-intensity ultrasound being applied to the wrist to raise the internal temperature and reduce inflammation. Several weeks of using this ultrasound device will probably relieve many of the symptoms of carpal tunnel syndrome, including pain, but it's also important for you to discontinue the repetitive hand motions during this period and perhaps even use a wrist splint while sleeping at night.

✔ **Yoga**: Yes, this is another Mayo Clinic idea. We've seen how a yoga practice can be effective with other types of pain. In the case of wrist pain, many yoga positions involve stretching the tendons and joints and this could help the wrist by strengthening it to relieve the pressure on the wrist nerve.

Treatment with Vitamins

✔ **Vitamin B6**: Nutrition and health expert Dr. Neal Barnard declared in his book *Foods That Fight Pain* how "the answer to carpal tunnel syndrome could lie in a simple vitamin— vitamin B6, also called pyridoxine. Its analgesic properties are commonly used to increase resistance to pain for people who are withdrawing from overused headache remedies and for people with nerve pains of diabetes and temporomandibular joint pain."

There are studies to support Dr. Barnard's point of view. He cites a series of them which found vitamin B6 deficiencies in patients diagnosed with carpal tunnel syndrome. Once vitamin B6 supplements were administered over a period of weeks, many of these patients reported fewer or no symptoms. Normally the treatment dose is 50-150 mg a day and this should be continued for up to 12 weeks as you monitor your symptoms and their severity.

It's also recommended that you consume foods rich in vitamin B6 as both a treatment and preventative measure. Beans, bananas, nuts, and whole grains are known to be rich sources of this important vitamin. Avocado and Brussels sprouts are two more food sources.

Other Supplements

- ✔ **St. John's wort** is sometimes a naturopathic medical suggestion for pain and inflammation reduction. It may also be useful to repair nerve damage. Try taking 250 mg of the extract three times a day and monitor the results.

- ✔ Herbal Rub: Another home remedy is to rub your wrists with a quarter teaspoon of arnica ointment. Do this twice a day. The anti-inflammatory nature of arnica may help ease the pain symptoms.

18 Natural Techniques for Pain Relief

If you are a normal human being you probably have released some swear words during your life when you hurt yourself and felt a surge of pain. Maybe you just exclaimed 'damn' or 'crap' or 'gosh darn it', if cuss words aren't in your vocabulary, but you undoubtedly let some verbiage fly.

Scientists tell us it's a good thing if we curse or shoot out a few choice words when we hurt ourselves because what we're really doing is releasing natural pain relievers fueled by emotion from our brain. Believe it or not, there are even studies documenting this effect.

In an August 2009 study report in the journal *NeuroReport,* a group of 67 student volunteers in Britain were told to keep their hands immersed in cold water for as long as they could stand it. When the students would begin vocalizing curse words, they were able to tolerate the pain an average of 40 seconds longer than if they stayed quiet.

"I would advise people, if they hurt themselves, to swear," commented psychologist Richard Stephens, who led the study, in an interview with *Scientific American*. Brain circuitry linked to emotion seems to be the key. It's that emotion which seems to play a role in dampening the sensations of pain and reducing the fear of experiencing pain.

Swearing is a short term remedy for pain, since you can't really keep your emotions high enough for hours on end to keep swear words effective as pain modulators. It's a little like another of our natural tendencies when we first experience a burst of pain— putting your hands to the painful area to compress it and briefly override the pain signals. That natural reflex, too, had a short-term pain reduction benefit.

Fear and anxiety magnify the effects of pain. If you are someone who is prone to catastrophizing—defined as always assuming a worst possible outcome in most situations—then the studies indicate you will probably experience the severity of pain you fear and expect. Fear and anxiety magnify the effects of pain. So in many respects, managing your pain really is at the heart of it, a mind game. It's back to what I said at the beginning of this book: pain begins and ends in your mind.

The power of your mind—and that includes faith and the prayers which help to sustain it—should never be underestimated when you are trying to manage chronic pain. You don't need to be one of those firewalkers, someone who walks across hot coals and resists the pain through mind focus alone, to utilize what nature has gifted each of us—the power to heal ourselves.

What I have sketched for you below is a variety of 'mind tools' to assist you in your quest for pain-free wellness. (While medical marijuana isn't strictly a technique, it does have an effect on the mind.) These natural practices and substances have had their effectiveness verified through trial and error over time, or through rigorous study in medical science laboratories.

You may want to combine the use of multiple pain relief tools into a sort of holistic daily program of healing for yourself. To give you some examples, you might create a ritual of watching a funny movie that makes you laugh, followed by a sauna, and then follow that up with a massage, followed by a mindfulness meditation. Or you could listen to soothing music while doing gentle yoga, and then getting an acupressure massage with aromatherapy while listening to more soothing music.

The possibilities of what you can create for yourself in combining these pain relievers are limited only by your imagination. Experiment with combinations of them. Try on different ways of being with yourself and with your pain management.

You will find what works best for you.

You have nothing to fear and nothing to lose but your pain.

Acupuncture (acupressure and reflexology)

What is it? These three pain relief tools—acupuncture, acupressure, reflexology—all basically evolved from the same fundamental Chinese medicine concept of energy meridians existing in the human body, with pressure points correlating to organs in the body. Each technique now has its own particular approach to healing and its own community of practitioners.

Acupuncture is the most ancient Chinese practice and has achieved widespread acceptance among Western medical practitioners, including the U.S. National Institutes of Health, for its ability to relieve the symptoms of a wide range of ailments, including pain. The application of tiny, thin needles at strategic areas of the body is based on the idea that the human body contains a meridian of energy or pressure spots which can be stimulated to correct imbalances that cause health problems.

How is it done? Typically an acupuncture practitioner will do an examination of you beforehand, looking at the shape and coloration of your tongue, taking your pulse on both arms, noting the smell of your breath, and other indicators which may seem strange to you. Based on this information and a description from you of your symptoms, a decision will be made as to where the small needles will penetrate your skin. Sometimes the needles are attached to a device that generates small electrical pulses into the body. Your entire session might last for just 10 minutes or for up to an hour, depending on the practitioner's diagnosis.

If you decide to undergo acupressure instead of using needles, much of the procedure is the same except that the practitioner uses hand or elbow pressure on the meridian points to obtain the desired result. You can also choose to undergo electroacupuncture, which is the application of a tiny electrical current into the acupuncture points.

What is the evidence for it? Skeptics of acupuncture like to say that any perceived benefits come from either the needles activating the brain's release of opioids, or from the patient's own expectations, otherwise known as the placebo effect. However relief from pain comes, let's examine some of the medical study evidence for the benefits available to you. Literally thousands of studies of acupuncture have been conducted, mostly by scientists in China.

✔ **Breast and Lung Cancer Pain**: The effects of foot reflexology on cancer pain received testing in patients with breast and lung cancer. Twenty-three patients aged 65 years and older were included in reflexology of both feet for 30 minutes done by a certified reflexologist.

Results: Not only did all patients experience "a significant decrease" in anxiety, patients with breast cancer "experienced a significant decrease in pain." January 2000, *Oncology Nursing Forum*.

✔ **Chronic Pain**: Electroacupuncture, the application of a tiny electrical current into acupuncture points, "blocks pain by activating a variety of bioactive chemicals through peripheral, spinal, and supraspinal mechanisms." These include the release of the brain's natural opioids. Studies indicate this procedure alleviates both sensory and inflammatory pain and inhibits neuropathic pain. Furthermore, this team of four researchers found, in evaluating the medical literature, "that electroacupunture, when combined with low dosages of conventional analgesics, provides effective pain management which can forestall the side effects of often-debilitating pharmaceuticals." February 2014, *Anesthesiology*.

✔ **Fibromyalgia**: In this review of studies done on acupoint stimulation (as done by acupuncture and acupressure) a total of 16 randomized clinical trials were evaluated involving 1,061 participants with fibromyalgia.

Results: This meta-analysis of studies found "that acupuncture alone or combined with cupping therapy was superior to conventional medications on reducing pain scores…… acupoint stimulation appears to be effective in treating fibromyalgia compared with medications." December 2013, *Evidence Based Complementary Alternative Medicine*.

✔ **Menstrual Pain**: A group of 32 women were involved in this study testing the effects of acupressure on menstrual pain and distress. (Acupressure uses the same body position points as acupuncture.)

Results: Acupressure was found to "have value in alleviating menstrual pain and menstrual distress in a high-stress life." December 2013, *Evidence Based Complementary Alternative Medicine*.

✔ **Migraine Headaches**: A total of 218 patients with persistent migraine headaches were involved in this study to test the effects of acupuncture applied in one session over 24 hours. One group was given real acupuncture treatment while a second group was administered 'sham' (fake) acupuncture.

Results: Real acupuncture was effective whereas sham acupuncture was not. "Acupuncture is clearly effective in relieving pain and preventing migraine relapse or aggravation," concluded the study authors. June 2009, *Headache*.

✔ **Neck Pain**: To determine how effective acupuncture has been in clinical trials for neck pain, one of the three most frequently reported complaints of the musculoskeletal system, a team of seven scientists examined the results from 10 studies that used acupuncture treatments for chronic neck pain.

Results: "There is moderate evidence that acupuncture relieves pain…and moderate evidence that acupuncture is more effective than inactive treatments for relieving pain post-treatment and this is maintained at short-term follow-up." July 2006, *Cochrane Database System Review*.

✔ **Neuropathy (peripheral)**: Certain chemotherapies given during cancer treatment cause peripheral neuropathy in cancer patients and this persistent pain impairs the patient's quality of life. In this study, 18 cancer patients with neuropathy were given a course of six weekly acupuncture sessions.

Results: After the sessions, 82% of the patients reported an improvement in their pain levels and other symptoms. Some also reported a reduced need for pain medications and improved sleeping patterns. September 2011, *Acupuncture Medicine.*

✔ **Osteoarthritis (knee):** In this study 160 knee osteoarthritis patients were divided into two groups: a therapy group that tested acupuncture once a day combined with heat-sensitive moxibustion applied around knee joints, and a Western medication group using glucosamine sulfate capsules (two capsules three times a day) along with sodium hyaluronate and triamcinolone acetonide acetate injections.

Results: After five weeks of treatment "results in the combined therapy {acupuncture} group was superior remarkably to the Western medication group." At a six-month follow-up, the acupuncture patients still had less pain and better knee function than the Western medicine group. There also were many fewer adverse reactions in the acupuncture group. September 2011, *Acupuncture Medicine.*

✔ **Shingles:** A total of 102 patients with severe pain from shingles (herpes zoster) were divided into two groups. One group received acupuncture treatment for four weeks while the second group got standard pharmacological treatments.

Results: The acupuncture group received as much pain relief as did the standard drug treatments, and acupuncture worked without any adverse side effects. "This controlled and randomized trial provides the first evidence of a potential role of acupuncture for the treatment of acute herpetic pain." June 2011, *BMC Complementary Alternative Medicine.*

Biofeedback

What is it? Suppose you could diminish or eliminate pain and sleeplessness simply by placing the focus of your attention on the area of pain or on the impediments to your good sleep, and then activate your mind to remedy the problem? Wouldn't you be inclined to try out this approach to see if it works for you?

Many people who use the various biofeedback techniques claim they can accomplish this mind over matter effect because biofeedback enables you to measure your bodily processes and conveys that information to you in real time. As your awareness of your body is raised, you begin to gain conscious control over some physiological activities that are normally automatic.

A biofeedback machine monitors everything from your skin temperature to your heart rate. By seeing the readings simultaneously as you feel the sensations, you learn to mentally control both the readings and the sensations until you can accomplish this without being hooked to any biofeedback device.

When you use temperature biofeedback, for instance, it can help you to treat some circulatory disorders and reduce the frequency of migraine headaches. Among other conditions successfully treated with biofeedback training: incontinence, chronic indigestion, Attention Deficit Hyperactivity Disorder, backaches, neck pain, fibromyalgia, the rehabilitation of motor skills in stroke victims and in people suffering from multiple sclerosis, and in the treatment of Parkinson's disease symptoms.

How to do it? If you consult the experts associated with the Association for Applied Psychophysiology and Biofeedback, which you can find on the Internet, the steps involved in mastering this at-home technique are presented. It will first involve having a session with a biofeedback technician, then learning to monitor the physical sensations on your own. These experts will also describe how to use biofeedback along with self-hypnosis to evoke the placebo response in a way that creates a powerful synergy for you to harness in dealing with pain.

What is the evidence for it?

✔ **Chronic Pain**: People with spinal cord injuries often experience chronic pain. In this study of 13 persons with spinal cord injury they were given four sessions each of three different neurofeedback (biofeedback) procedures.

Results: All three biofeedback variations "had similar immediate effects on pain intensity…the participants reported modest pre- to post-treatment decreases in worst pain and pain unpleasantness following completion of the 12 sessions. These improvements were maintained at 3-month follow-up." June 2013, *Applied Psychophysiological Biofeedback*.

✔ **Fibromyalgia**: To determine the effect of biofeedback exercises on pain from fibromyalgia, researchers did a meta-analysis of seven published studies involving 321 fibromyalgia patients.

Results: "In comparison to control groups, biofeedback significantly reduced pain intensity with a large effect size." September 2013, *Evidence Based Complementary Alternative Medicine*.

✔ **Headache (chronic)**: Ten children with chronic headaches attending an outpatient pediatric neurology clinic practiced relaxation with biofeedback and "learned to associate successful relaxation with positive pain-free virtual images of themselves."

Results: "Ratings of pain, daily functioning, and quality of life improved significantly at 1 and 3 months post-treatment." May 2013, *Pain Medicine*.

✔ **Neck pain**: Thirty secondary school teachers aged 25 to 45 years with neck pain received training in pressure biofeedback; a control group got conventional exercise therapy only.

Pain measurements were taken before the study and after two and four weeks of training.

Results: More improvement in pain and disability was experienced by the biofeedback group. June 2013, *Journal Physical Therapy Science.*

✔ **Osteoarthritis (knee)**: A total of 30 persons with knee osteo-arthritis were divided into two experimental groups. Group A received EMG biofeedback, knee muscle strengthening exercises, and did Iyengar yoga for eight weeks. Group B did the EMG feedback and exercises without yoga.

Results: "Patients in both groups experienced significant reduction in pain and improvements in functional ability." July 2013, *International Journal of Yoga.*

Chiropractic Medicine

What is it? As an alternative to pharmaceutical painkillers, many people choose to have their backaches and joint aches treated by a doctor of chiropractic medicine. Founded in the late 1890s, its practitioners diagnose and treat problems with the musculoskeletal system of your body, particularly your spine.

Procedures of manual manipulation used by chiropractors overlap with osteopathy, massage therapy and physical therapy. Some chiropractors focus almost entirely on adjustments of the spine, others treat the spine, joints, and soft tissues and include other treatments, such as the the use of herbal supplements.

How to do it? Journalist Randall Fitzgerald in his 2006 book, *The Hundred Year Lie: How to Protect Yourself from the Chemicals that are Destroying Your Health,* described the pain he felt after an injury and how narcotic painkillers did nothing to quell the pain, whereas a session with a chiropractor made the pain disappear within minutes.

"I slipped and fell during a snowstorm. When I hit the street curb, I took the full force of impact on the right side of my lower back. The next day, my injury and pain was exacerbated by a cramped three-hour flight home to California. The throbbing sensation in my lower back became so severe that my body began slipping into shock. Friends rushed me to the emergency room of a hospital, where I was hooked up to an intravenous morphine drip. The morphine barely dulled my sensation of pain. X-rays for broken bones were negative, and an attending physician speculated that the fall had bruised one of my kidneys. He wrote me a prescription for a strong narcotic painkiller and sent me home with the confession that "there is nothing else that can be done for you." The emergency room visit cost seven hundred dollars. Though I debated whether to fill the prescription because of my concern about the narcotic's potential for disorientation and addiction, the discomfort was so constant and intense, magnified by my every movement, that I could not imagine that I had any other choice.

"As I walked in agonizing pain to a neighborhood pharmacy, I happened to pass by a chiropractic clinic. Though I had no reason to believe that a chiropractor could provide relief, my intuition urged me to at least inquire. A middle-aged chiropractor attended to me immediately and applied a heat compress to my lower back, followed by an ultrasound treatment. She then spent 10 minutes doing deep tissue massage on the affected area. She explained how these manipulations combined with heat and sound—a synergistic effect—would help to restore the internal alignment of my kidney. Her technique worked like magic. I got off the table and my pain was instantly and completely gone, and it never returned. The session only cost fifty-five dollars, and the experience sold me on the idea that the synergistic effects of natural treatments and remedies can be effective and economical."

What is the evidence for it?

✔ **Neck Pain**: Researchers gathered together the results from 27 study trials conducted assessing whether neck manipulation, such as that performed by chiropractors, lessened pain.

Results: "Moderate quality evidence" showed that cervical manipulation lessened pain in neck pain patients. August 2010, *Manual Therapy*.

✔ **Low Back Pain**: Studies of chiropractic spinal manipulation, cognitive behavioral therapy, massage, acupuncture, and yoga for low back pain treatment were collected as had published through 2006, and these were compared and analyzed.

Results: "We found good evidence that **cognitive behavioral therapy** and **spinal manipulation** are all moderately effective for chronic or sub-acute low back pain. We found fair evidence that **acupuncture, massage and yoga** are also effective for chronic low back pain." October 2007, *Annals Internal Medicine*.

✔ **Migraine Headaches**: Twenty-two studies involving 2,628 patients aged 12 to 78 years were compared and assessed for which non-invasive treatments work best for chronic headaches.

Results: For the treatment of migraine headache "there is evidence that spinal manipulation may be an effective treatment option." July 2004, *Cochrane Library*.

Cognitive Behavioral Therapy (CBT)

What is it? If you are able to change your beliefs about pain, you can change your relationship to pain. That means controlling the intensity of it. CBT uses the idea that your thoughts can both obstruct your ability to heal from an injury, or can be used to enhance your capacity to heal. CBT teaches you to identify negative or irrational beliefs that make your pain worse. It's a variation on the 'mind-over-matter' approach to managing or eliminating pain.

How to do it? Working CBT with a trained therapist, you can regulate the emotions which contribute to your pain by identifying what is motivating your thoughts and behaviors. You learn to trace the cause and effect pattern in your mind that contributes to compulsive thoughts and behaviors that trigger or intensify pain.

What is the evidence for it? Studies have shown the potential of CBT to assist you in relieving painful conditions.

✔ **Joint Pain**: University of Washington School of Medicine researchers found CBT to be effective in reducing chronic temporomandibular disorder pain (this is the joint connecting the mandible to the skull).

Results: Study participants in the CBT group experienced three times higher levels of pain intensity relief than patients in a control group who didn't use CBT. April 2006, *Pain*.

✔ **Abdominal Pain**: Children suffering from chronic abdominal pain were studied. Twenty-nine of these kids were randomly placed into two groups, a control group without CBT and a group which used six sessions of CBT.

Results: "Children in the intervention group experienced both a reduction in pain and an improvement in health-related quality of life compared to the control group. The effect sizes ranged from medium to high." February 2012, *International Journal of Behavioral Medicine*.

✔ **Chronic pain**: Using a variation of CBT called cognitive restructuring, a team of German researchers examined its effects on 109 female students who were exposed to thermal pain stimuli. Those in the cognitive restructuring experimental group were trained to change how they thought about the pain to improve their ability to cope with it. The other participants were taught how to practice acceptance of the pain and a third group used distraction techniques to shift their attention away to lessen their pain levels. All of these methods are variations of CBT.

Results: Those who accepted their pain condition were best at tolerating pain, whereas those in the distraction and cognitive restructuring groups also better reduced their pain perceptions. Cognitive pain management strategies can be useful in the treatment of chronic pain, concluded the scientists. April 2013, *The Journal of Pain*.

✔ **Fibromyalgia**: A group of girls aged 8 to 17 years were treated for symptoms of juvenile primary fibromyalgia using cognitive behavioral techniques (progressive muscle relaxation and guided imagery) to reduce pain and facilitate sleep.

Results: "In the majority of patients such techniques were effective in reducing pain and facilitating improved functioning." October 1992, *Journal of Rheumatology*.

✔ **Low Back Pain**: Studies of chiropractic spinal manipulation, cognitive behavioral therapy, massage, acupuncture, and yoga for low back pain treatment were collected as had published through 2006, and these were compared and analyzed.

Results: "We found good evidence that **cognitive behavioral therapy** and **spinal manipulation** are all moderately effective for chronic or sub-acute low back pain. We found fair evidence that **acupuncture, massage and yoga** are also effective for chronic low back pain." October 2007, *Annals Internal Medicine*.

Far-Infrared Sauna

You probably know how a traditional sauna works. The air is heated and this in turn heats up your body to produce sweating. The higher the heat and the longer you stay in the sauna room, the more you perspire.

What is it? With an Infrared sauna, also called a far-infrared sauna, infrared heaters release infrared light and this radiant heat is absorbed by the surface of your skin. The heat penetrates several inches into your body and this penetration, according to its advocates, enables your body to release toxins and also provides pain reduction benefits which traditional saunas do not provide.

What is the evidence for it? Various studies from throughout the world, particularly Japan, have demonstrated some effectiveness by infrared saunas in lessening the pain associated with fibromyalgia, chronic fatigue syndrome, rheumatoid arthritis, and chronic pain conditions.

- ✔ **Chronic Pain:** Two groups of chronic pain patients were involved in this study. Group One, consisting of 24 patients, had their chronic pain treated by a combination of cognitive behavioral therapy, rehabilitation, and exercise therapy. Group Two, consisting of 22 patients, were all treated with far-infrared-ray dry sauna therapy and post-sauna warming once a day for four weeks.

  Results: Pain scores for both groups "decreased significantly" after treatment; however, two years after treatment, 77% of the infrared group was able to return to work compared to 50% in the multidisciplinary treatment Group One. 2005, *Psychotherapeutic Psychosomatic.*

- ✔ **Fibromyalgia:** In this Japanese study 13 female fibromyalgia patients, age range 25 to 75, received far-infrared-ray dry sauna treatments once a day for 15 minutes. Afterwards they were covered with a blanket from the neck down for 30 minutes.

Results: "All patients experienced a significant reduction in pain by about half after the first session." August 2008, *Internal Medicine*.

Guided Imagery

What is it? There is quite a bit of evidence from medical science studies showing the benefits of using a sequence of soothing images before bedtime to quiet your mind and relax your body for rest.

Maybe you have had already had experience with its effects and didn't realize it. A good example is if you've had the experience of daydreaming at work. Maybe it's in the middle of winter, and you are imagining yourself on a tropical beach. You imagine you can feel the warmth of the sun and the salt air on your skin and you can sense the waves gently lap at your feet. Suddenly, you realize this image is so vivid that your skin has actually heated up. It could even be hot to the touch. Your imagination was harnessed showing you how it is a powerful tool for healing and for controlling your body, including your ability to get good sleep.

How to do it? At the Academy for Guided Imagery neuro-scientists teach how to use guided imagery to lessen your illness symptoms and to enhance your immune system functioning. This practical, low-cost and easy to use tool has proven effective for lots of self-care, particularly among cancer patients, because imagery helps the body to release endorphins, its own natural painkillers.

A review by the American Cancer Society of 46 studies on imagery and cancer revealed that it was effective for reducing pain, stress, depression, and other side effects associated with cancer treatment.

What is the evidence for it?

✔ **Headaches**: Researchers did a guided imagery experiment with 129 patients suffering from chronic tension-type headaches.

Results: The visualization intervention group reported "significantly more improvement" in all measurements of pain after each session and after one month of the guided imagery tape therapy. May 1999, *The Journal of Head and Face Pain.*

✔ **Fibromyalgia**: A group of 55 women with previously diagnosed fibromyalgia pain were divided into two groups. One received relaxation training and guided instruction in how to generate pleasant imagery in order to distract themselves from their pain. A control group received treatment as usual.

Results: Concluded the study authors: "Pleasant imagery was an effective intervention in reducing fibromyalgia pain during the 28-day study period." May 2002, *Journal of Psychiatric Research.*

✔ **Pain Sensation**: A group of female volunteers in long term romantic relationships were shown photos of their romantic partners while they received painful stimulation; women in a control group received the same painful stimulation while they viewed photos of strangers. Participants of both groups had the prefrontal cortex of their brains scanned during the experiment.

Results: Those who viewed photos of their romantic partners had "reduced pain ratings and reduced pain-related neural activity." The longer the relationships and the greater perceived partner support translated into more pain tolerance. June 2011, *Proceedings of the National Academy of Sciences.*

✔ **Osteoarthritis Pain**: A group of 30 senior citizens suffering from osteoarthritis pain went through a four-month clinical trial of guided imagery.

Results: Their guided imagery use reduced pain levels and lowered prescribed arthritis medication use. The study authors were so impressed they urged pain management physicians to incorporate guided imagery in their toolbox of treatments. March 2010, *Pain Management Nursing.*

Homeopathy

What is it? It's the idea that 'like cures like'. Something which causes a health condition is used to heal similar symptoms in an ill person. A homeopathic remedy is made from herbs or flowering plants and then diluted until no molecules from the original substance can be detected. Homeopaths believe the water which held those molecules retains a 'memory' of them and that is the trigger for your body's own natural healing mechanisms to kick into action.

Mainstream medicine regards homeopathy as quackery. To the extent any health benefits result from taking a homeopathic remedy, it is said to be a placebo effect, the power of belief to heal. There have been dozens, if not hundreds, of clinical studies testing homeopathic remedies and the results have been mixed, to say the least.

Well-known oncologist and homeopath Dr. James Forsythe identified the most popular and proven pain-relief remedies used by homeopaths. Here are his top five pain relievers:

✔ **Arnica**: Some homeopaths declare that this substance can be highly effective in battling the excruciating pain of **arthritis**. Arnica comes from an herb derived from a yellow flower that grows at high elevations in Europe. Patients using arnica apply this on their skin in the form of a gel, or they take it orally.

✔ **Curcumin**: This spice used widely in India helps to lessen or prevent painful swelling. Your body will usually absorb curcumin better if you take it orally as a capsule. Also called turmeric, curcumin is an anti-inflammatory useful in battling symptoms of **arthritis**. This spice does have a lot of study support for its therapeutic effects.

✔ **Devil's Claw**: If you have any stomach problems you are advised to avoid this remedy which is taken from a fruit that grows in South Africa; it is often found effective in treatments for **backaches** and **arthritis**.

✔ **Feverfew**: Homeopaths use this flowering plant which is found all across North America, Europe, and the Mediterranean to generate a medicinal herb—often considered helpful in getting relief from the pain of **headaches** and **arthritis**.

✔ **Frankincense**: Frankincense is an aromatic resin from the boswellia trees in Armenia and is used in perfumes and incense. Frankincense can be eaten in pure form and has been a treatment used for hundreds of years to treat **arthritis pain**. It may also be useful in treating **ulcerative colitis** and **Crohn's Disease**, those intestinal inflammatory conditions.

Humor Therapy

It's no secret that humor can be a powerful weapon in your arsenal of pain-fighting tools, if only you would choose to consciously and consistently harness it.

To understand why laughter seems to relieve pain symptoms in most if not all people, a team of scientists in Britain did a series of six experimental studies with groups of volunteers that involved watching funny videos or watching comedic stage performances in person. Afterwards the scientists measured to what extent laughter had lessened pain sensations.

Bear in mind part of the reason for this study was to evaluate the effects of 'social laughter', which is to say, how laughter within a group of people can intensify its physiological effects well beyond what laughing alone can do. The study authors observed how previous research had indicated that "laughter is 30 times more likely to occur in social contexts than when alone."

To induce some level of pain in the study participants without injuring them, a device called "a frozen vacuum wine cooler sleeve" was applied to their arm. In another of this series of studies the participants had pain induced using a strenuous exercise routine. They were tested using funny movies and stage performances and then tested again by being shown dramas without any humor-inspiring laughter.

Here is what the study authors concluded: "Results show that pain thresholds are significantly higher after laughter......this pain-tolerance effect is due to laughter itself." Laughter induced "an endorphin-mediated opiate effect" on pain levels, a euphoric state, perhaps because of the muscular exertion involved in belly laughs." September 2011, *Proceedings of the Royal Society B: Biological Sciences*.

This study added to a growing body of scientific evidence that laughter is really good for your health. To fight pain it's advisable to laugh with others and make that laughter as contagious as possible to get the maximum benefit, though you will also still get pain relief if you experience laughter by yourself.

Want more evidence? Here are a few more studies to get you motivated.

✔ **Chronic Pain**: "Humor therapy: relieving chronic pain and enhancing happiness for older adults." Researchers took 36 people in a nursing home and placed them into an eight-week humor therapy program; 34 other people were put in a control group who weren't given the humor program.

Results: The study authors concluded: "Upon completion of the humor therapy program, there were significant decreases in pain and significant increases in happiness and life satisfaction for the experimental group, but not for the control group. The use of humor therapy appears to be an effective non-pharmacological intervention." June 2010, *Journal of Aging Research*.

✔ **Pain Tolerance**: "Laughter, humor, and pain perception in children: a pilot study." In this study done at UCLA a group of 18 children aged 7 to16 years watched humorous videos before, during, and after a standardized pain task was administered. Pain severity ratings and pain tolerances were recorded at each stage of the study.

Results: The researchers discovered that the kids who were exposed to humor "demonstrated significantly greater pain tolerance while viewing funny videos." June 2009, *Evidence Based Complementary & Alternative Medicine*.

"Humor as a cognitive technique for increasing pain tolerance." In this rather clever study, 80 persons were divided into four groups of people with 20 test subjects in each. One group was shown a humorous film, the second viewed a repulsive film, the third saw a neutral film, and the fourth group did no film screening at all. Pain tolerances were tested using a process called cold pressor stimulation.

Results: Both the humor and repulsive movie groups "showed a significant increase in pain tolerance as compared to the other groups." (As a general rule, you're probably much better off choosing the funny film over the repulsive one so you don't trigger bad dreams or toxic thoughts.) November 1995, *Pain*.

Hypnosis

What is it? Just before you fall asleep you enter a slightly hypnotic state. You may also find yourself entering it when you're deeply immersed in a tedious task or in reading a particularly engrossing book. Daydreaming is another way to experience this state of mind which is trancelike.

Most of us enter what can be called trance states numerous times during the daily routine of our lives. Dr. Larry Dossey calls hypnosis a window into the soul of healing and that statement receives support from hundreds of medical studies showing how hypnotic states and self-hypnosis can alleviate health symptoms and even help to cure some types of health maladies.

Not everyone can be hypnotized so this technique isn't for everyone. There is still debate about what being in a hypnotic state really means. Though hypnotic subjects remain fully awake, they become more responsive to suggestions made to them, though not to the extent they would do anything out of character. This suggestibility (which may be related to the placebo effect) is why hypnosis can be a useful tool in short-circuiting pain signals.

What is the evidence for it? Since 2003, physicians at a Belgian hospital, Cliniques Universitaires St. Luc in Brussels, have been offering surgical patients the option of choosing hypnosis rather than general anesthesia when undergoing surgery and then experiencing the resultant pain during recovery. Thousands of patients have chosen the hypnosis option in Belgium, and many more in

Britain where it is used during dental surgery, and in Germany where it is used by facial surgeons.

At the Brussels hospital which has been pioneering the use of hypnosis in surgery, about one-third of all surgeries to remove thyroids and one-quarter of all breast cancer surgeries use hypnosis. Major operations such as heart surgery don't use it because the dangers are greater, but procedures like hernias and knee arthroscopies are good candidates for the technique.

✔ **Surgical Pain**: A clinical trial in the U.S. conducted by a team of 11 scientists randomly assigned 200 women scheduled to undergo excisional breast biopsy or a lumpectomy to 15 minute pre-surgery hypnosis sessions or a session with a psychologist in which they simply listened. Patient-reported pain was measured after the procedures.

Results: Patients in the hypnosis group reported less pain intensity and required fewer medications in the aftermath of surgery. "The present data support the use of hypnosis with breast cancer surgery patients," reported the study authors. September 2007, *Journal of the National Cancer Institute*.

"You have to be in the right mental frame of mind for this," warned one of the Belgian patients in an interview with Associated Press. "If you're very skeptical of hypnosis and freaked out about whether it's going to work, it probably won't."

Other medical research has demonstrated how hypnosis can accelerate the healing of bone fractures and reduces the pain associated with broken bones, cutting down on the need for medications. Self-hypnosis also can reduce anxiety after coronary bypass surgery and facilitates faster healing and a reduction in pain medication requirements. Studies have also shown how burn wound healing undergoes "dramatic enhancement" when hypnosis is used.

✔ **Chronic Pain**: In this study researchers tested the effects of self-hypnosis on individuals with multiple sclerosis who were experiencing chronic pain.

Results: The University of Washington researchers concluded that their findings "supported the greater beneficial effects of self-hypnosis training on average pain intensity." January 2011, *The International Journal of Clinical & Experimental Hypnosis.*

This study tested the effect of self-hypnosis (rather than hypnosis induced by a hypnotist) combined with muscle relaxation on multiple sclerosis (MS) patients who experienced chronic pain. Twenty-two MS patients were involved and one group of them was taught how to use self-hypnosis.

Results: "General hypnotizability was not significantly related to treatment outcome, but treatment outcome expectancy assessed before and after the first session was. The results support the efficacy of self-hypnosis training for the management of chronic pain in persons with MS. Gains were maintained at 3-month follow-up." April 2009, *The International Journal of Clinical & Experimental Hypnosis.*

✔ **Fibromyalgia**: Five Spanish scientists published the results of their study of fibromyalgia patients and hypnosis in which they combined its use with Cognitive Behavioral Group Therapy. Ninety-three fibromyalgia patients were randomly assigned to one of three experimental groups.

Results: The group using hypnosis and therapy had far better outcomes than the other groups as measured on pain severity measurement scales. January 2012, *Journal of Pain.*

Massage

If you have touched yourself at the site of an injury immediately following that injury, such as burning your hand on a stove, you may have experienced a momentary lessening of the pain. Intrigued by this phenomenon, some British scientists decided to investigate this effect under experimental conditions.

They gathered a group of volunteers and subjected them to limited pain using thermal grill illusion, a lab method for studying pain perception. The volunteers had their index and ring fingers placed in warm water while their middle finger was immersed in cold water, which gives people the sensation of the middle finger being painfully hot. That way pain could be studied without actual injury to the participants in the study.

Pain in their middle finger dropped by an average of 64% when study participants touched the three fingers of one hand to the same fingers of the other hand, and did so immediately following the onset of a pain sensation. What was apparently happening, the study authors wrote in a September 2010 issue of *Current Biology*, is that the human brain took all of the tactile sensation signals and integrated them into a single experience which reduced the pain severity back towards normal.

The healing power of touch to give us comfort and pleasure is wired into our brains and nowhere is that power better illustrated than in our natural ability to reduce chronic pain. That brings us to massage and the benefits of receiving touch from another human being.

Research was produced by Canadian scientists and featured in a February 2, 2012 article in *Science* magazine showing that getting a massage reduces the levels of a chemical in your body which triggers the genes associated with inflammation in your body.

✔ **Back Pain:** In a study assessing alternative medicine treatments for back pain a large team of researchers evaluated several hundred randomized controlled trial studies, one of them was massage.

Results: "Massage was superior to placebo or no treatment in reducing pain and disability amongst subjects with acute/sub-acute low back pain. Massage was also significantly better than physical therapy in improving back pain." October 2010, *Evidence Reports/Technology Assessments.*

This same study above also concluded that "for subjects with **neck pain**, massage was better than no treatment, placebo, or exercise in improving pain or disability."

✔ **Cancer Pain:** Thirty cancer patients with bone metastases were involved in this study testing the effectiveness of massage in reducing pain.

Results: "Massage therapy was shown to have effective immediate, short-term, intermediate, and long-term (more than 16 hours) benefits on pain intensity." April 2009, *Journal of Pain Symptom Management.*

✔ **Low Back Pain:** Studies of chiropractic spinal manipulation, cognitive behavioral therapy, massage, acupuncture, and yoga for low back pain treatment were collected as had published through 2006, and these were compared and analyzed.

Results: "We found good evidence that **cognitive behavioral therapy** and **spinal manipulation** are all moderately effective for chronic or sub-acute low back pain. We found fair evidence that **acupuncture, massage and yoga** are also effective for chronic low back pain." October 2007, *Annals Internal Medicine.*

Medical Marijuana

Step by step and year by year, medical marijuana has garnered mainstream acceptance as a pain reliever in many parts of the U.S. and other countries. It's challenging to keep up anymore with which states have adopted medical marijuana use laws or which states have decriminalized pot use because the changes in public opinion and state laws are so rapid.

What is it? Marijuana is considered 'natural' because it grows wild in nature and the plant has been used therapeutically for thousands of years. It's probably the most widely used 'illicit' natural drug on the planet.

When we discuss marijuana and pain relief it's important to first define our terms. The two main compounds of marijuana are cannabidiol (CBD) and delta-9 tetrahydrocannabinol (THC). It is the THC which acts as the psychoactive ingredient in pot, giving users their high.

Much of the medical science research has focused on the entire class of cannabionids in the marijuana plant, such as what is found in smoked or eaten cannabis, extracts of cannabis, nabilone, dronabinol, and THC analogues developed by chemists. Generally (aside from the obvious toxic effects of smoke on the lungs when pot is smoked), these substances have been found to be mostly safe and effective for some forms of chronic pain.

Here is a summary of a few studies and their findings:

✔ In one experiment 21 men and women suffering from a range of conditions, including arthritis, inhaled vaporized marijuana three times a day. They were already taking daily doses of either morphine or oxycodone to treat their **chronic pain.**

Results: Study participants achieved a 25% additional reduction in their pain index levels. Keep in mind the study participants were experiencing severe chronic pain from their medical conditions, so the therapeutic use of marijuana, according to the study authors, provides hope "that marijuana could someday be used as a replacement for narcotics to help curb some of the side effects associated with those medications." December 2011, *Clinical Pharmacology and Therapeutics.*

✔ A review of the medical literature was done to assess the usefulness of medical cannabis formulations for dealing with various types of **pain** and **muscle spasticity.**

Results: "Studies of medical cannabis show significant improvement in various types of pain and muscle spasticity." February 2013, *Pharmacotherapy.*

✔ For this study 23 persons, average age of 45 years, all of whom had post-traumatic or postsurgical **neuropathic pain**, were assigned to receive cannabis at four potencies (0%, 2.5%, 6%, and 9.4% tetrahydrocannabinol) over four 14-day periods. They inhaled a single 25 mg dose through a pipe three times daily.

Results: "A single inhalation of 25 mg of 9.4% tetrahydrocannabinol herbal cannabis three times daily for five days reduced the intensity of pain, improved sleep, and was well tolerated." The cannabis preparation of less potency "yielded intermediate but non-significant degrees of relief." October 2010, *Canadian Medical Association Journal.*

Meditation

What is it? To clear your mind and experience the 'power of now', you don't need to be a yogi master or a believer in an Eastern religion. Meditation can be part of a spiritual practice, but it is also a safe and simple technique to enhance your health and overall well-being, to bring about faster healing after illness or injury, and to put you in a state of mind to make restful sleep more possible.

Meditation practices are being prescribed and successfully used for such conditions as anxiety, stress, skin diseases, infertility, chronic pain, high blood pressure, insulin levels, heart attack and stroke prevention, immune system stimulation, obsessive-compulsive disorder, depression and other psychiatric conditions. Because meditation helps to relax both the body and mind, it is a natural and effective approach for your self-treatment of sleep problems.

By slowing your breath and quieting your mind, you can bring about deep relaxation and learn to tap into your body's own inner healing wisdom. Though numerous meditation techniques exist—such as Vipassana, Kriya, and Transcendental Meditation, many medical researchers, like University of Wisconsin neuroscientist Richard Davidson, use combinations or variations on all of the techniques. (Once again, we have touched on a theme of this book—try out combinations of remedies for best results.)

It's well known that anxiety and stress can increase pain intensity. So anything that naturally decreases anxiety and stress can have positive effects on pain symptoms. If you add feelings of loving-kindness or a practice of forgiveness to a meditation technique, you actually increase the benefits related to pain management, according to numerous studies.

How to do it? The general steps of how to go about meditating and integrating that practice into your life can be found by doing an Internet search (try 'meditation' or 'mindfulness meditation') detailed by experts in easy to understand language. You will find YouTube videos online that take you through the steps of using meditation for pain relief. There are many meditation techniques, too many to give examples of in these pages. (Also see in the Appendix of this book several meditations created by psychotherapist Donald Altman.)

What is the evidence for it?

✔ **Low Back Pain**: At Duke University Medical Center, a team of seven researchers used a loving-kindness meditation, designed to transform anger into compassion, with 43 patients suffering from chronic low back pain. The program lasted eight weeks.

Results: The study confirmed "significant improvements in pain and psychological distress" among those in the loving-kindness group. By letting go of resentments and anger associated with traumas, people or events, pain sufferers are better able to cope with pain because they have released the triggers that intensify pain. September 2005, *Journal of Holistic Nursing*.

✔ **Fibromyalgia**: A review of studies done on the clinical effects of meditation on fibromyalgia and cancer pain found "the quality and quantity of valid research is growing...... Meditation practice can positively influence the experience of chronic illness," including fibromyalgia and the simple technique for mindfulness can be taught in any clinical setting. November 2003, *Holistic Nursing Practice*.

One experimental study took 28 fibromyalgia patients and put them through eight sessions of a combined treatment which included meditation training, cognitive behavioral therapy, and Qigong, the Chinese movement therapy.

Results: "Significant improvement was seen...in a range of outcome measures including tender points and pain threshold. Improvement was sustained 4 months after the end of the intervention." August 2000, *Arthritis Care Research*.

Mindfulness

What is it? It's been said that the state of mindfulness is like standing on a metaphorical subway platform and clearly and calmly observing each 'car' of the subway train as it passes by—each thought, opinion, sensation, and emotion—*without* jumping on that subway train and riding it down the track.

Think of mindfulness as a moment-to-moment attentiveness where you pay attention to your thoughts, your feelings, your sensations, your perceptions, your opinions, your memories; whatever may be happening in your life, you do the mindfulness without judgment or rejection or blaming anyone. In many ways it's the opposite of stress, you know, that worried, unsettled, past- and future-fixated state of mind that releases hormones like cortisol and adrenalin that undermine good health.

How to do it? Being able to harness our mental awareness to reduce stress and fight illness and disease was an idea that was brought into the medical mainstream by Jon Kabat-Zinn, a Professor of Medicine emeritus at the University of Massachusetts. He is also the founding executive director of the Center for Mindfulness in Medicine, Health Care, and Society. Dr. Kabat-Zinn describes how there are two ways to bring mindfulness into your life:

Try mastering it through a formal meditation practice, carving out time each day to be alone, and then to drop into an inward silence and stillness.

You can also practice it by remembering to bring a spacious, moment-to-moment, non-judgmental awareness to every situation you find yourself in during your day. This is called *informal* mindfulness practice—and it's much easier to do this when you are also practicing formally on a regular basis.

"The most important thing to remember about mindfulness meditation is that it is about paying attention non-judgmentally in the present moment," says Dr. Kabat-Zinn. "We emphasize the present moment because that is the only time any of us are alive. The past is over, the future hasn't happened yet, and the only way we can effectively influence the future is by living fully and consciously in the moments in which we are actually alive, which is always NOW."

To try a mindfulness meditation technique, assume a comfortable posture lying on your back or sitting. If you're sitting, keep your spine straight and let your shoulders drop. Close your eyes. "The easiest and most effective way to begin practicing mindfulness as a formal meditation practice is to simply focus your attention on your breathing and see what happens as you attempt to keep it there," says Dr. Kabat-Zinn.

What is the evidence for it? Studies show that a mindfulness technique called "Mindfulness-Based Stress Reduction" can reduce the burden of many different diseases and health conditions, including pain and sleep-related issues. It works by relieving the underlying stress that plays a role in the onset of these health issues and intensifies the symptoms once they appear.

> ✔ **Arthritis**: To assess the effect of Mindfulness-Based Stress Reduction on symptoms associated with rheumatoid arthritis, 31 people attended an eight-week Mindfulness course and 32 others became the control group, who had no exposure to Mindfulness.
>
> **Result**: "At 6 months there was significant improvement in psychological distress and well-being, and marginally significant improvement in depressive symptoms" in the Mindfulness group, as opposed to the control group, and "a 35% reduction in psychological distress among those treated." October 2007, *Arthritis Rheumatism.*

✔ **Back Pain**: A study of 37 adults aged 65 years and older with moderate intensity back pain suffered daily participated in an eight-week Mindfulness program with periodic assessments of pain, physical function, and quality of life. They used the program technique an average of 31 minutes a day, an average of four days a week.

Result: At the end of the intervention the group "displayed significant improvement" in the lowering of pain, in physical function, and overall quality of life. February 2008, the journal *Pain*.

✔ **Fibromyalgia**: Fifty-eight females with fibromyalgia were divided into a Mindfulness group, or a social support group in this Swiss study. During the eight-week programs, both groups were monitored for three types of pain associated with fibromyalgia.

Result: Mindfulness provided "significantly greater benefits than the control intervention," and a three-year follow-up of mindfulness group participants found "sustained benefits" for all three pain measures. 2007, *Psychotherapy Psychosomatics*.

✔ **Menopausal Pain**: Fifteen women who had entered menopause and were experiencing frequent and severe hot flashes spent eight weeks in Mindfulness-Based Stress Reduction classes at the University of Massachusetts Medical School. They kept a daily log of their hot flash occurrences.

Result: Hot flash severity "decreased 40%" and "women's scores on quality-of-life measures increased significantly." September/October, the journal *Menopause*.

Music Therapy

What is it? We've all had the experience of music being a source of relaxation no matter what our musical taste happens to be. When it comes to using music to help relieve your pain, study evidence indicates that you need to emphasize melodic music that will soothe and calm you, not arouse you mentally and physically.

Generally speaking, classical music has been found to work this soothing and calming effect more effectively than any other style of music (rap or hard rock, for instance), but what works best really depends on your own tastes in music. (Singing or playing an instrument can also have a soothing effect on your pain level, though there is much less study evidence than for music-based therapies that involve listening.)

What is the evidence for it? There is a lot of persuasive study evidence for the role that music can play.

- ✔ **Knee Osteoarthritis**: In one study the researchers placed 62 patients undergoing joint lavage for knee osteoarthritis into one of two groups—a group which received no music intervention, and a second group which listened to recorded music. Median age was 68 years old for the study participants; two-thirds of them were women.

  Results: The findings were unequivocal: "Music is a simple and effective tool to alleviate pain and anxiety in patients undergoing joint lavage for knee osteoarthritis." December 2011, *Clinical Rheumatology*.

- ✔ **Spine Surgery Pain**: A second study looked at the effects of music therapy on 60 patients who were receiving spine surgery. The study participants listened to selected music from the evening before their surgery through the second day after the surgery was performed.

Results: The findings showed positive results: "Music therapy can alleviate pain and anxiety in patients before and after spinal surgery." April 2011, *The Journal of Clinical Nursing*.

✔ **Osteoarthritis**: In a third study a group of people with an average age of 50 were recruited from pain and chiropractic clinics in Ohio. They suffered from the painful conditions of **osteoarthritis, disc problems, and rheumatoid arthritis** and had been in chronic pain for up to six years. Those in the study listened to music on a headset an hour a day and kept a pain diary. A control group didn't listen to the music but also kept a pain diary. The music used was piano, jazz, orchestral, and harp.

Results: Those listening to music reported pain severity decreased by up to 21%, where those in the non-music group felt their pain increased. Those in the music group also reported more mental control over their pain symptoms. September 2006, *Journal of Advanced Nursing*.

A team of French scientists used music therapy with 87 patients suffering from lumbar pain, fibromyalgia, inflammatory disease or neurological disease. They received at least two daily sessions of music and on returning home from the hospital, continued the music intervention. "This music intervention method appears to be useful in managing chronic pain as it enables a significant reduction in the consumption of medication," the research team concluded. October 2011, *The Clinical Journal of Pain*.

To evaluate the effects of music on pain levels in cancer patients, scientists evaluated 30 clinical trials conducted on 1,891 cancer patients. In 17 of the studies the patients listened to prerecorded music, while in the remaining studies they actually took part in guided music therapies with song, piano playing or other expressions. The review of studies concluded: "This systematic review indicates that music interventions may have beneficial effects on anxiety, pain, mood, and quality of life in people with cancer." August 2011, *Cochrane Database System Review.*

Music is so potent a healer that an entire field of medical professionals have emerged using music therapy and sharing study results in their own medical journal, *The Journal of Music.*

Qigong

What is it? You may have some trouble pronouncing the word, Qigong ('chi-kung') but beyond the name, anyone can benefit from this ancient Chinese practice because it uses your body posture, your breathing, and your ability to create visualizations to activate your general health maintenance and to treat a variety of health conditions, including pain.

There are two styles of Qigong. One is called external Qigong therapy because it involves interaction between a patient and a trained Qigong healer. The second approach is internal Qigong therapy where you undertake individual practices and exercises without interaction with someone else.

Anyone can learn the practice of Qigong to maintain or improve your health. Medical experts in Qigong can be found on the Internet who will walk you through the basic steps of how to begin a Qigong practice. These websites can also tell you where to turn to for professional guidance and training. You may even undertake the ancient practice only to decide that you wish to deepen your experience of it by taking it to another level.

Many of the studies done on Qigong and pain have involved combining it with meditation and/or deep breathing and other natural practices, so evaluating Qigong on its own isn't always easy and the results have been mixed.

What is the evidence for it?

✔ **Fibromyalgia**: Fourteen fibromyalgia patients were randomly assigned to one of two treatment groups. The experimental group did a six-week Qigong exercise regimen that included meditation and deep breathing. The second control group did a 'sham' (fake) Qigong exercise for six weeks.

Results: No effects were seen in the control group, but in the Qigong group the researchers found it to be "a potentially effective self-management approach in controlling" fibromyalgia symptoms, particularly pain. November 2012, *International Journal of Neuroscience*.

A second study had 20 persons with fibromyalgia do a 60-minute per day training for eight weeks as pain assessments were made every few weeks.

Results: Qigong practice "led to significant improvements in pain, impact, sleep, and physical function in the 13 subjects who completed the trial." These changes were maintained at the six-month level. August 2013, *Evidence Based Complementary Alternative Medicine*.

✔ **Osteoarthritis**: A team of scientists in Texas evaluated studies which had been done on Qigong, Tai Chi and yoga in treating pain and other symptoms associated with osteoarthritis.

Results: They found "some studies in China reported improvement of severe arthritis symptoms," including a reduction in pain. July 2011, *Arthritis*.

Relaxation Response

What is it? You don't always know when stress is stalking you. It can creep up on you over time, a shadow that grows larger until it brazenly overpowers your mind and body like a mugger in broad daylight. Your immune system falls prey first, rendering you vulnerable. Insomnia is often a byproduct of stress that is out of control.

Stress is the number one trigger for illness and disease. The relaxation response is a self-help therapeutic technique which can help. It involves repeating a word, sound, prayer or other phrases (much like a mantra) as you sit quietly in a comfortable position, your eyes closed, as you breathe slowly, relaxing each part of your body. You do this for 10 to 20 minutes twice a day. You can also use visual imagery to heighten this relaxation effect.

Harvard Medical School Professor Herbert Benson, founder of the Mind/Body Medical Institute, created the relaxation response four decades ago. It's a deceptively powerful yet simple way to strengthen your immune system or to treat many stress-connected disorders and diseases. When activated, your metabolism slows, as do your heartbeat and breathing, and your muscles relax and the levels of nitric oxide in your body increase.

What is the evidence for it?

✔ **Headache**: A review was conducted of the results from several hundred studies examining the relaxation response.

Results: It was found that headaches and insomnia were two of the more effective treatments for which the technique can be used. 2001, the *Journal of Alternative and Complementary Medicine*.

✔ **Fibromyalgia**: A variation on the relaxation response is slow, deep breathing (yogic breathing) and this was tested in 27 women with fibromyalgia as they were exposed to low and moderate thermal pain pulses.

Results: "Slow breathing reduced ratings of pain intensity." April 2010, *Pain*.

✔ **Migraines**: Eighteen children between the ages of 8 and 12 were studied for the effect that relaxation response training would have on their migraine headaches over 15 weeks.

Results: The treatment group "experienced a significant reduction in headache symptoms" and this reduction in headache symptoms was maintained one year after treatment ended. April 1986, *Developmental Medical Child Neurology.*

✔ **Premenstrual Syndrome Symptoms**: Over five months the effects of the relaxation response on 46 women and their premenstrual symptoms, including pain, was assessed.

Results: "We conclude that regular elicitation of the relaxation response is an effective treatment for physical and emotional premenstrual symptoms and is most effective in women with severe symptoms." Those with severe symptoms saw a 58% improvement. April 1990, *Obstetrics & Gynecology.*

Tai Chi

What is it? It began in China and remains popular there, which is why you may have seen photos or videos showing groups of people, quite often elderly Chinese, standing together outdoors in parks, and moving slowly and rhythmically as if they were taking a martial arts class. This moving meditation, called Tai Chi, is a 'soft' martial arts technique. It is intended for the practitioner to use their mind to train their body for health enhancement.

How to do it? You don't need to become a Tai Chi expert to receive benefit from the practice. There are many websites which provide useful advice on how to integrate a Tai Chi practice into your life for the best results. Solo routines can be done (you don't always need to be part of a group) and even solo you can pick up the series of movements which can be learned naturally, by placing an emphasis on your coordination while in relaxation.

As with the other relaxation techniques described in the pages of this book, Tai Chi is a tool which is often best used in combination with other pain-reducing suggestions.

What is the evidence for it?

✔ **Osteoarthritis**: A team of scientists in Texas evaluated studies which had been done on Qigong, Tai Chi, and yoga in treating pain and other symptoms associated with osteoarthritis.

Results: They found five randomized controlled trials which documented Tai Chi as "significantly reducing pain intensity in osteoarthritis patients." July 2011, *Arthritis.*

✔ **Fibromyalgia**, Low Back Pain, Osteoarthritis: In a review of study evidence for Tai Chi in relieving pain for a variety of chronic pain conditions, the author focused on five pain conditions. Of these, three had supporting evidence.

Results: "Tai Chi seems to be an effective intervention in osteoarthritis, low back pain, and fibromyalgia." July 2012, *Anesthesia Pain Medicine.*

✔ **Shingles**: A total of 112 older adults aged 59 to 86 were given Tai Chi classes for 25 weeks to evaluate the effect on resting and vaccine-stimulated levels of cell-mediated immunity to varicella zoster virus (shingles).

Results: The Tai Chi group compared to a health education control group boosted the effectiveness of a vaccine against the shingles virus and "the Tai Chi group also showed significant improvements in score for bodily pain." April 2007, *Journal of American Geriatric Society.*

Yoga

What is it? Don't be fooled by what you thought you knew about it. Yoga isn't just a series of movements that some people use for exercise, and it isn't just a spiritual practice used by New Agers trying to find bliss. Yoga means 'union', and that's exactly what practitioners of yoga attempt to do—unite their mind and body and spirit through movement to enhance their overall vitality and maintain their health.

Since at least the second century B.C., when oral and written records indicate that yoga first came about as a mind-body system of health in India, its physical postures and breathing exercises have been regarded by its practitioners through the ensuing centuries as having a positive impact on their overall health.

You should probably experiment to choose a style of yoga practice that best suits your physical condition and health needs. Yoga experts online and associated with yoga studios can describe simple breath control exercises, called pranayamas, to aid digestion and sleep induction.

The basic body postures and movements in yoga are known as asanas. Yoga reference sources can be found on the Internet so you can embrace a style of yoga practice in more depth using widely available educational books and videos, including YouTube.

What is the evidence for it?

✔ **Osteoarthritis**: A team of scientists in Texas evaluated studies which had been done on Qigong, Tai Chi, and yoga in treating pain and other symptoms associated with osteoarthritis.

Results: They found studies showing that Iyengar yoga, emphasizing strength, flexibility and relaxation, is a practice that "has been shown to reduce pain" in osteoarthritis patients. July 2011, *Arthritis.*

Another study focused just on Iyengar yoga and had volunteers over the age of 50, all with knee osteoarthritis, do 90-minute classes once a week for eight weeks.

Results: "Statistically significant reductions in pain" were observed and no adverse effects occurred as a result of doing the yoga. August 2005, *Journal of Alternative and Complementary Medicine.*

✔ **Chronic Back Pain**: In this study 228 healthy adults with moderate chronic back pain were randomly assigned to one of three study groups. One group took weekly 75-minute yoga classes, the second group did stretching exercises, while the third just read a book on back pain.

Results: Both yoga and stretching flexibility exercises produced an improvement in back pain resulting in a decreased use of pain medication. October 2011, *Archives of Internal Medicine.*

✔ **Fibromyalgia**: Canadian scientists testing how to reduce symptoms of chronic pain in women with fibromyalgia had the study participants do a program of 75 minutes of hatha yoga twice weekly over a period of eight weeks.

Results: Practicing yoga reduced the symptoms of chronic pain in the women. It was the first study to evaluate the effect of yoga on elevating cortisol levels in the body, which seems to be the natural chemical mechanism by which pain is reduced following a yoga workout. July 2011, *Journal of Pain Research.*

✔ **Osteoarthritis (knee)**: A total of 30 persons with knee osteoarthritis were divided into two experimental groups. Group

A received EMG biofeedback, knee muscle strengthening exercises, and did Iyengar yoga for eight weeks. Group B did the EMG feedback and exercises without yoga.

Results: "Patients in both groups experienced significant reduction in pain and improvements in functional ability......adding Iyengar Yoga along with conventional therapy provides better results in chronic unilateral knee osteoarthritis in terms of pain and functional disability." July 2013, *International Journal of Yoga*.

✔ **Low Back Pain**: Studies of chiropractic spinal manipulation, cognitive behavioral therapy, massage, acupuncture, and yoga for low back pain treatment were collected as had published through 2006, and these were compared and analyzed.

Results: "We found good evidence that **cognitive behavioral therapy** and **spinal manipulation** are all moderately effective for chronic or sub-acute low back pain. We found fair evidence that **acupuncture, massage, and yoga** are also effective for chronic low back pain." October 2007, *Annals Internal Medicine*.

Top 12 Herbal, Food and Vitamin Pain Remedies

In alphabetical order (based on study results and numbers of pain-related conditions effectively treated).

- ✔ **Alpha-lipoic acid** — Diabetic neuropathy, Headache, Nerve pain.

- ✔ **Capsaicin (red pepper)** — Arthritis, Back pain, Diabetic neuropathy, Neck pain, Shingles, Toothache.

- ✔ **Cherries (tart)** — Arthritis, Gout, Osteoarthritis.

- ✔ **Curcumin (a curry spice)** — Arthritis, Muscle pain, Neuropathy, Rheumatoid Arthritis.

- ✔ **Echinacea** — Earache, Sore throat, Toothache.

- ✔ **Evening Primrose** — Arthritis, Headache, Premenstrual syndrome, Rheumatoid arthritis.

- ✔ **Garlic** — Arthritis, Earache, Migraines.

- ✔ **Ginger** — Back pain, Headache, Migraines, Muscle pain, Osteoarthritis, Rheumatoid Arthritis, Toothache.

- ✔ **Glucosamin and Chondroitin** — Arthritis, Joint pain, Osteoarthritis, Rheumatoid arthritis.

- ✔ **Licorice** — Acid reflux, Shingles, Sore throat.

- ✔ **Omega-3 fatty acids** — Arthritis, Nerve pain (neuropathy), Premenstrual syndrome, Rheumatoid arthritis.

- ✔ **Peppermint** — Back pain, Endometriosis, Sunburn.

The 18 Natural Practices and the Pains They Treat

✔ **Acupuncture** — Breast cancer pain, Chronic pain, Fibromyalgia, Menstrual pain, Migraines, Neck pain, Neuropathy, Osteoarthritis, Shingles.

✔ **Biofeedback** — Chronic pain, Headache, Fibromyalgia, Neck pain, Osteoarthritis.

✔ **Chiropractic Medicine** — Back pain, Migraines, Neck pain.

✔ **Cognitive Behavioral Therapy** — Abdominal pain, Back pain, Cancer pain, Chronic pain, Fibromyalgia, Headaches, Insomnia, Joint pain, Menopause, Tooth Extraction.

✔ **Far-Infrared Sauna** — Chronic pain, Fibromyalgia.

✔ **Guided Imagery** — Arthritis, Cancer pain, Chronic pain, Fibromyalgia, Fractures, Headaches, Insomnia, Osteoarthritis, Tooth Extraction, Wounds.

✔ **Homeopathy** — Arthritis, Backache, Headache.

✔ **Humor Therapy** — Chronic pain.

✔ **Hypnosis** — Chronic pain, Fibromyalgia, Surgical pain.

✔ **Massage** — Back pain, Cancer pain.

✔ **Medical Marijuana** — Cancer pain, Chronic pain, Muscle pain, Neuropathy.

✔ **Meditation** — Back pain, Cancer pain, Fibromyalgia, Menopause, Tooth pain.

✔ **Mindfulness** — Arthritis, Back pain, Fibromyalgia, Menopausal pain.

✔ Music Therapy— Burns, Osteoarthritis (knee), Rheumatoid arthritis, Spine surgery, Toothache.

✔ **Qigong** — Cancer pain, Fibromyalgia, Osteoarthritis.

✔ **Relaxation Response** — Headache, Fibromyalgia, Migraine, Premenstrual Syndrome.

✔ **Tai Chi** — Back pain, Fibromyalgia, Headache, Menopause, Osteoarthritis, Shingles.

✔ **Yoga** — Back Pain, Cancer pain, Chronic Pain, Fibromyalgia, Insomnia, Menopause, Multiple Sclerosis pain, Osteoarthritis, Premenstrual Syndrome, Rheumatic Diseases.

PART TWO

Sleep is the First Casualty of Pain

18 Natural Sleep Enhancers

It's said that truth is the first casualty of war. The first casualty of pain is sleep and when it is impaired, there goes your peace of mind.

Without adequate sleep—not just rest, but deep slumber—we all know how irritable we can get, how tired we feel, and how cloudy our awareness and clarity of mind becomes. Prolonged sleep disruption degenerates vital neurons in the brain and results in the buildup of proteins associated with premature aging and neural degenerative diseases like Alzheimer's. Being sleep deprived depresses your immune system and makes you more susceptible to illness and disease.

Pain in any form and at any level, but particularly chronic pain, is the most powerful and devious saboteur of good sleep.

Your sensitivity to pain, the level of pain you can tolerate, is also directly connected to the amount of sleep—restful sleep—you get each night. In the medical journal *Sleep* a study was published (December 2012) that got right to the heart of the matter.

Sensations of pain were decreased by 25% in study subjects who slept just two hours longer than other persons aged 21 to 35 who participated in the experiment and got less sleep. This measurement was based on a pain tolerance test given to the study subjects. Believe it or not, that amount of improvement in pain tolerance was greater than the effects 60 milligrams of codeine had on pain sensitivity. That just goes to show how powerful our own natural pain suppression system and its capacity can be.

"Our results suggest the importance of adequate sleep in various chronic pain conditions or in preparation for elective surgical procedures," said study co-author Dr. Timothy Roehrs. He and fellow study scientists suspect that sleep disruption and sleep restriction trigger the release of cytokines in the body, which are stimulants for developing the inflammation that produces pain sensations or which intensifies your experience of already existing pain conditions.

So your tolerance for pain and your sleep habits are bedfellows, so to speak. The less sleep you get the more pain you feel; the more pain you feel the less sleep you get. How to break that vicious cycle to restore balance to your life? That's a central question I will attempt to answer in this book.

If your answer is to reflexively pop one of those pharmaceutical sleeping pills for a quick fix, you are lost and on the wrong path in a health wilderness, according to many sleep researchers. Science writer Maria Konnikovajan wrote an insightful article for *The New York Times* (Jan. 11, 2014) about research on getting a good night's sleep, in which she observed: "The sleep researchers I spoke with agree that there's no evidence that aided sleep {use of sleeping pills} is as effective as natural sleep."

Getting your quota of natural sleep and doing so while you are in the grip of pain means using natural sleep remedies whenever you can. Otherwise, the side effects of Big Pharma's 'magic' pills and quick fixes can undermine your long term health and peace of mind.

Because pain is such a disruptive force and sleep can be such a fragile enterprise, it's important for you to know what natural remedies for sleep are most effective and which ones are best suited to rebalancing your own unique sleep cycle. You will find some of the answers for yourself in this section of the book.

> Drug-induced sleep isn't a truly restful or healthy anti-aging sleep.

What Sleep Relief Does Big Pharma Offer?

Being constantly sleep deprived isn't 'normal', but neither is taking sleeping pills. Both ways of being have documented serious side effects and both degrade your overall quality of life.

Big Pharma's answer to every problem is to pop a pill. Their answer to sleep deprivation caused by pain is to offer up highly addictive medications and they urge you to replace one with another as the effects diminish over time. You've probably heard of some with names like Seconal, Luminal, Amytal, Dalmane and Tranxene. Overdose on them and you can die.

Dr. James Forsythe summed up the effects of these drugs this way: "Sleeping pills that come to you via prescriptions don't just put you into a prolonged sleep. They do their job by affecting your entire central nervous system. They are knockout drugs. You wake up the next morning feeling drugged because you have been drugged. You have been in a condition comparable to being comatose and you haven't experienced normal sleep cycles during the night. Needless to say, this sort of 'sleep' experience over time isn't healthy. Sleeping pills manufactured from synthetic chemicals are NOT safe when used in the long term. Dependency develops. Other side effects can appear. Drug-induced sleep isn't a truly restful or healthy anti-aging sleep."

Three Categories of Prescription Sleeping Pills

Whether you take prescription sleeping pills or not, it would be useful to know some of the basics about what Big Pharma has to offer and their possible health risks to users.

Benzodiazepine: Xanax, Ativan, and Valium are sleep drugs that focus on affecting your central nervous system. Usually prescribed as sedatives and for anxiety, they can be risky for developing dependence or addiction. There are negative effects reported with long term use which include depression, irritability, nausea, and even in some cases, amnesia.

Non-Benzodiazepine: Ambien, Sonata, Lunesta, and Zolnod are among the brand name medications in this class of sleep drugs. These are known to have risks associated with users developing physical or psychological dependence. That is a danger from long term use. There may also be risks of memory impairment after frequent or longer term use.

Antidepressants: Desyrl and Risperdal are among a group of antidepressants sometimes prescribed because their tranquilizing effects are thought to help induce sleepiness in patients. This is where 'Off-label' prescribing comes in. That means a physician has prescribed an antidepressant for a sleep problem though that particular drug wasn't manufactured with this type of use in mind.

When Dr. Forsythe advises his patients to use sleeping pills as a last resort, not as the first resort, I am there cheering him on.

How Much Sleep Is Enough?

For years we've all heard the mantra from mainstream medical authorities that we each need eight hours of restful sleep a night. But is that really true? Is sleep a one-size-fits-all conditioned behavior?

Not everyone has the same set of physical requirements for sleep, just as we all have different pain thresholds and different sensitivities to drugs and foods. Albert Einstein was said to need 10 hours of sleep a night for his clarity of mind, yet another scientific genius, the inventor Thomas Edison, claimed he got by just fine with only four or five hours of sleep.

The National Sleep Foundation makes a case that the key to having sleep that is restful is to prevent disruptions of the fourth stage of your deepening sleep cycle known as REM—rapid eye movement. The first three stages of sleep are preparation for REM and you go through these cycles numerous times in a normal night of sleeping.

In stage one you are sleeping lightly and can be easily awakened. When you drift into a deeper stage you are no longer aware of conscious thoughts. Next you enter deep sleep and if you are awakened, you feel grogginess and maybe slight disorientation. Once you make the transition into stage four, REM sleep, your breathing is more rapid and shallow, your eyes move back and forth behind your eyelids, your legs and arms feel paralyzed, and your blood pressure goes up. On awakening from this REM sleep stage you can more readily remember your dreams and those dreams seem more vivid. This four-stage sleep cycle keeps repeating throughout the night and research indicates that REM and the delta brain wave transition leading into it are the most important stages to experience in feeling rested once you are awake.

Six REM Sleep Saboteurs To Avoid

1. **Pain**. Needless to say, avoiding or reducing sensations of pain is a must, which is where the first part of this book can assist you. These other sleep saboteurs conspire with pain, so you will need to arrest them as well.

2. **Alcohol**. Drinking alcoholic beverages before bedtime may help you to fall into the first stage of light sleep, but alcohol sabotages your ability to reach stage four REM sleep and to remain there for the necessary length of time.

3. **Caffeine**. Any caffeinated drink, whether it is coffee, tea or energy drinks, will have effects in your body system lasting for hours and that can induce insomnia or light sleep stages only. The same effects hold true for nasal decongestants or diet pills.

4. **Nicotine**. The effects of nicotine in your body are well documented, and, like caffeine, impairs your ability to reach the REM stage of sleep and to remain there. A good indication that you are being REM sleep deprived is if you have difficulty remembering your dreams.

5. **Antidepressants**. The neurotransmitter signals in your brain that regulate REM sleep are susceptible to disruption by the chemicals in antidepressant drugs.

6. **Temperature Extremes**. Your sleeping environment plays an important role. Too much heat or too much cold where you sleep tampers with your body's ability to regulate body temperature and that, in turn, robs you of vital REM sleep.

Most surveys done on sleeping habits indicate that women experience far more sleep disruptions than men, by an average of 58% to 48%. Chronic pain is the primary culprit. Pain discomfort reportedly interrupts these women's sleep three nights and more a week and the most common pain conditions are tension headaches, arthritic and rheumatic disorders, heartburn, and migraines. Other culprits include premenstrual syndrome and, later in life, menopause.

Everyone should keep in mind, most especially women, that sleep deprivation and any reduction in the quality of sleep can produce weight gain and obesity. That's another sort of painful reality about sleep habits. The National Sleep Foundation has framed the dilemma this way: "People who don't get enough sleep are more likely to have bigger appetites due to the fact that their leptin levels (leptin is an appetite regulating hormone) fall, prompting appetite increase. This link between appetite and sleep provides further evidence that sleep and obesity are linked. To top it off, the psychological manifestations of fatigue, sleep, and hunger are similar. Thus, when you're feeling sleepy you might feel like you need to head for the fridge instead of bed."

...sleep deprivation linked to your risk of developing obesity, it's a strong indicator that you could contract Type 2 diabetes...

Not only is sleep deprivation linked to your risk of developing obesity, it's a strong indicator that you could contract Type 2 diabetes with all of its health consequences and drugs prescribed by mainstream medicine. Research done at the University of Pennsylvania Perelman School of Medicine examined the effects sleep deprivation can have on mice and their cellular functions. Both young and old mice experienced cellular stress and increases in their blood glucose levels when deprived of sleep, but the older ones showed by far the most negative changes. When your normal glucose metabolism is disrupted, you invite diabetes into your life. While this research was done on mice, the results easily translate to human beings. The physiological principles are the same in both mice and humans.

Six Emotions That Sabotage Sleep

Living with pain often produces insomnia, and your thoughts surrounding these conditions, if they become obsessive, can add another element to this combustible mix. The more fixated you become on your pain and insomnia, the more anxiety and intense emotions your body absorbs. It's another one of those recurring vicious cycles that I underscore in this book as being important to break.

To sever the links in that cycle you can teach yourself, using practical relaxation techniques, how to short-circuit the impact of those obsessive thoughts and relax your body to make restful sleep more possible. To start this process, let's take a look at the emotions which may come up when struggling with the insomnia that often attaches itself to chronic pain.

1. **Anxiety** – It only seems natural that you would feel anxious about the pain you feel and the lack of sleep you experience as a result. Add to that the normal stresses of ordinary life and anxiety can become a constant state of distress.

2. **Anger and Frustration** – As the pain/insomnia cycle continues, feelings of anger and frustration may boil just beneath the surface until periodic eruptions occur. This can negatively impact your personal and business relationships if you don't find healthy coping mechanisms. If you have difficulty expressing anger, your mind may keep churning out agitated thoughts.

3. **Depression** – Many folks end up battling depression during bouts with chronic pain and insomnia. It's also a consequence of long-term use of painkiller drugs. Any prolonged and severe depression needs professional treatment.

4. **Hopelessness** – Who wouldn't feel that hope for relief has slipped away when gripped by out-of-control pain and insomnia? This is another reason why I felt this book was necessary. There is hope if only we will open our eyes and minds to it.

5. **Panic** – Any uncontrolled anxiety can result in panic attacks. The mind-calming exercises detailed in this book can help, but if the episodes continue or become more intense, you may need to seek professional counseling.

6. **Worry** – If you can't 'turn off' your thoughts when you need sleep, and you are constantly projecting into the future, your overall stress level goes up and that makes insomnia worse. Of course, this can also happen even in the absence of a pain condition, so that makes the relaxation exercises a more universal remedy for sleep deprivation.

Later in this section of the book you will find a series of relaxation techniques which have been shown to be useful natural remedies for dealing with the seven emotions which contribute to sleep deprivation.

Are You In Denial About Sleep Loss?

If you experience sleep loss or sleep deprivation as a 'normal' condition, you may have adapted to your circumstances to a certain extent, but damage is still being done to your body and your mind. The National Sleep Foundation, which is a wonderful resource for everything having to do with sleeping, provides a series of questions you should ask yourself to determine if you are in denial.

✔ Do you need coffee or other stimulants every morning for alertness?

✔ Do you have difficulty remaining focused when sitting for long periods?

✔ Do you feel your moods turning more negative as the day goes on?

✔ Do you experience a fuzzier memory or sharpness toward the end of the day?

If you answered yes to two or more of the questions, The National Sleep Foundation says that you probably are experiencing a chronic sleep loss condition.

Insomnia is a chronic sleep loss condition and Dr. Helene A. Emsellem, medical director of The Center for Sleep & Wake Disorders, recommends detecting it by using this measure: "If you feel that you're getting an insufficient amount of sleep and it's happening on a regular basis, then we consider that to be insomnia. If you're having difficulty falling asleep or staying asleep – some individuals may fall asleep fine but wake up between two and five in the morning and not be able to sleep the final portion of the night. Any of these patterns may be considered insomnia."

What Happens When Your Sleep Suffers?

Medical science studies tell us that failing to get sufficient sleep directly impacts your health in a variety of ways. Here are a few of many examples.

✔ **More pain.** Getting four hours or less of sleep each day will increase the inflammation in your body. (Remember, inflammation results in pain.) This connection was found in test subjects by measuring levels of C-reactive protein, a marker which is also associated with an increased risk for developing coronary artery disease, in people deprived of adequate sleep. (*Journal of the American College of Cardiology.* 2004; "Effect of sleep loss on C-reactive protein, an inflammatory marker of cardiovascular risk." Meier-Ewert HK. Et. al.)

✔ **More susceptibility to illness.** Losing sleep depresses your immune system, a discovery verified in a study in which young adults were given a flu vaccination after undergoing four nights of abnormal sleep. Testing revealed that they had less than half of the antibody response than what was measured in a control group of test subjects who were given flu shots. (*Journal of the American Medical Association.* 2002; "Effect of sleep deprivation on response to immunization." Spiegel K. Sheridan JF. Van Cauter E.)

✔ **More cardiovascular problems**. By restricting your sleep duration to four hours or less a night, you raise your blood pressure and increase your heart rate, which are known markers for developing cardiovascular disease. (*Hypertension.* 1996; "Effects of insufficient sleep on blood pressure monitored by a new multibiomedical recorder." Tochikubo O. Ikeda A. Et. al.)

✔ **More risk for diabetes**. Four hours or less of sleep a night can trigger impaired glucose tolerance, which many studies have shown to be a risk factor for developing diabetes. (*Lancet.* 1999; "Impact of sleep debt on metabolic and endocrine function." Spiegel K. Et. al.)

✔ **More weight gain and obesity risk.** Chronic sleep deprivation, in which you get four hours or less a night, can produce increased appetite and that in turn promotes the onset of weight gain and eventual obesity. (*Annals of Internal Medicine.* 2004; "Sleep curtailment in healthy young men is associated with decreased leptin levels, elevated ghrelin levels, and increase hunger and appetite." Spiegel K. Et. al.)

✔ **More risk for a premature death**. A lot of research has been done indicating that compared to persons who sleep seven to eight hours a night, an increased risk of early death develops in persons who sleep much less than seven hours. (This also holds true for persons who sleep nine hours or more.) (*Journal of Sleep Research*. 2009; "Sleep duration and mortality: a systematic review and meta-analysis." Gallicchio L. Kalesan B.)

Other Contributing Factors to Sleep Loss and Insomnia

Like conspirators hatching a plot against your well-being, other protagonists periodically join forces with pain to disrupt your ability to get adequate restful sleep. Let's round up the usual (and unusual) suspects.

Watch Out for Sleep Apnea — When you get into your fifties and enter middle age, a fat buildup and loss of muscle tone usually occurs. If the fat buildup affects the area around your throat, your windpipe can gradually collapse as you breathe during sleep. This condition is obstructive sleep apnea and it's much more prevalent than you might have thought, affecting millions of people.

A fellow traveler with sleep apnea is snoring, an irritating condition most of us have to contend with at some point in later life, either because we do it or we must endure it from a partner. With obstructive apnea your air flow gets momentarily blocked for seconds at a time resulting in plummeting blood oxygen levels. That jolts you awake for a few moments. This cycle might occur hundreds of times throughout the night. No wonder folks with sleep apnea never feel fully rested during the day and find themselves prone to drowsiness and irritability. You may even wake up with a headache from all of that blood oxygen fluctuation in your brain.

If left untreated, sleep apnea can place you at risk for developing cardiovascular disease, stroke, congestive heart failure, depression, and memory loss. There have even been cases reported of sudden death from respiratory arrest.

"If you experience snoring on a regular basis and it can be heard from another room," says a National Sleep Foundation factsheet, "or you have been told you stop breathing or make loud or gasping noises during your sleep, these are signs that you might have sleep apnea and it should be discussed with your doctor."

If you have a mild case of sleep apnea the usual doctor recommended treatment is undergoing weight loss, along with changing your sleeping position from your back to habitual use of stomach and side of body sleeping positions. More severe cases of sleep apnea may require the use of masks designed to facilitate more regular breathing.

You might also try playing a musical instrument. As strange as it may sound, a 2006 issue of the *British Medical Journal* featured a study describing how in a test of 25 sleep apnea patients who were taught to play the Australian Aborigine instrument, the Didgeridoo, it was shown to be "an effective treatment well accepted by patients with moderate obstructive sleep apnea syndrome." It only took 25 minutes of practice a day for positive results to show up during sleep. Apparently, playing the instrument strengthened upper airway muscles making snoring less severe.

A final caution here is warranted. If you have diagnosed sleep apnea, sleep experts have warned that you shouldn't take sleeping pills or sedatives in general because they can have the effect of preventing you from waking up enough times during the night to breathe in the proper amount of oxygen your brain and body needs.

Watch Out for Restless Legs Syndrome — This neurological disorder involves the involuntary jerking and movement of the legs, a spasmodic response to feeling a prickly or tingly sensation in the feet or legs. It's most prevalent in people with diabetes or the elderly population. Insomnia frequently results from this disorder.

If we are to believe the sleep experts, perhaps 10% of people in the U.S., Canada, and Europe will experience some degree of restless legs syndrome during their life. Mainstream medicine usually tries to treat the condition by prescribing drugs that manipulate the levels of dopamine, a brain neurotransmitter.

Some other physical conditions that can disrupt your sleep include:

✔ Asthma.
✔ Gastroesophageal reflux disease.
✔ Immune system disorders.

Time to Fix Your Chronic Snoring

> Don't just give up and resign yourself to thinking that snoring is a condition you and your partner must live with until death.

Snoring is not only hazardous to your health, it disrupts the sleep and, by virtue of that, the health of those who sleep with and around you. Don't just give up and resign yourself to thinking that snoring is a condition you and your partner must live with until death. You aren't married to this condition. You have some options to treat chronic snoring and I would encourage you to try them out to see what works best for you.

✔ **You Need to Change Your Sleeping Position.** Sleeping on your back contributes to snoring because in that position gravity is pulling your throat area backwards, which disturbs air flow through your nostrils. Experiment with making a habit of only sleeping on your sides or your stomach. This may take time and practice and conscious effort.

There are a few techniques to try if you are having trouble staying off your back. Your sleeping partner can pinch you or nudge you when you are on your back and snoring, but that isn't fair to your partner because it interrupts their sleep. One trick for you to try is to wear a shirt or pajama top with a small ball sewn into a pocket at the middle of your backside. I challenge you to successfully sleep on your back when you feel this round obstruction poking you.

✔ **You Need to Lose Weight.** Always keep in mind your added pounds contribute to the fat tissue around your throat and that creates a snoring hazard risk. Obviously, there are lots of reasons to maintain a healthy body weight and snoring should always be considered one of them.

✔ **You Need to Stop Smoking.** Whether it's cigarettes, cigars, or marijuana joints, smoke is a throat irritant and a nasal membrane irritant. Smoke can trigger a snoring problem or make an already existing problem worse.

✔ **Two More Snoring Triggers**. Alcohol use before bedtime is a known snoring trigger; also, sedative medications tend to make snoring more chronic.

If you find that none of the solutions listed above are helpful to you, Mayo Clinic recommends that you graduate to the next level of treatment options. Here they are ranked from the cheapest and easiest to do on your own through the more expensive and more complex.

✔ **Snoring Reduction Medications**. Nasal saline sprays used before bedtime may moisturize your nasal lining and help to ease your snoring condition.

- ✔ **Breath-rite strips** are a cheap, low-tech device sold in drugstores and help to open up the frontal part of your nose. That should help reduce snoring but only if that area is the source of the problem. If this doesn't work, try out the next in your series of options.

- ✔ **Dental mouthpieces** are worn while you sleep and these help to shift the position of your tongue and soft palate. That movement helps to keep your air passage open. Other form-fitting dental devices will hold your jaw forward.

- ✔ **Palatal implants** are implants designed to create scar tissue which can stiffen your palate. It consists of braided strands of Dacron polyester filament which are injected into the soft palate. This can be useful but only if your soft palate is what causes your chronic snoring.

- ✔ **Continuous positive airway pressure**, a pressurized mask worn over your nose while sleeping, is often used on folks with obstructive sleep apnea. Connected by tubing to a small pump to keep air pressure high and constant, the mask helps to prevent airways from narrowing, which is a primary cause of snoring and sleep apnea.

- ✔ **Radiofrequency tissue ablation** may sound like a mouthful, but it uses low-intensity radio frequency signals to remove a part of the soft palate, which may decrease snoring. It's an outpatient procedure and only takes about 15 minutes. Two-thirds of people who have this procedure done say they experience less snoring.

- ✔ **Surgery** may be your last resort if the other procedures listed above don't work as advertised. One approach is to correct a deviated septum, that 'wall' separating the right and left nasal passages which loose cartilage can obstruct.

Nine More Tips for Sound Sleep

As compiled by sleep experts, groups, and organizations such as The National Sleep Foundation, what you will find in these nine tips are some common sense approaches that you are encouraged to experiment with, either individually or putting a group of them taken together, to see what works best for you.

You should create a sleep friendly bedroom.

Do you have a bedroom environment that is sleep friendly? Chances are you haven't even thought in these terms. Now is the time to examine what you have surrounded yourself with in your sacred sleeping space.

An obvious first step is to do whatever is necessary to keep your sleep space dark when you need it to be. That means heavier curtains if needed to keep out ambient light.

If necessary, practice using eye shades if you can't filter all of the external lights out. Even being exposed to subtle low lighting can be a sleep disrupter because light tricks your brain into semi-alertness. This can occur if you have the screen of a laptop computer on a night stand nearby or even a smart phone with any sort of illumination. Same thing holds for a neon-lit alarm clock. Keep in mind that light interferes with your body's natural production of the sleep hormone melatonin.

Light therapy for insomnia involves special lights that are brighter than your ordinary household light. These are timed to come on several hours before the time you might ordinarily wake up. This approach is supposed to help you adjust your biological clock for a regular sleeping cycle. It's sometimes used to treat the symptoms of jet lag.

Do you have noises around you that may interrupt your sleep? For example, a grandfather clock that ticks loudly and chimes at regular intervals, or other electronic devices that emit periodic beeps and alerts. You may need to experiment with wearing earplugs, especially if your partner snores loudly. Many people have found it useful to have 'White noise' sound machines in their sleeping area with breeze or ocean or waterfall sounds to soothe them for restful sleep.

It should be needless to say that an uncomfortable mattress, and lumpy or stiff pillows, can all contribute to sleep disruption.

You can develop a regular sleep cycle.

We all have an internal circadian 'clock' located in our brain that regulates our sleep cycle. It's a cycle that's easily disrupted. That's one reason why it's important to have a regular sleep ritual where you go to bed at a particular time and wake up at a regular time. This routine contributes to quality sleep.

Start developing that routine by waking up to the first rays of sunshine in the morning, or at least expose yourself to bright lights after waking up. This light exposure triggers your body to reset your biological clock every day.

There is some provocative research which indicates that your daily routine influences sleep quality, yet it may be dependent on your age. A December 2013 study in the *Journals of Gerontology* examined the sleep patterns of 100 persons—50 of them between the ages of 18 and 30, and 50 between 60 and 95 years of age.

All of the study participants kept a daily diary of when they performed activities during the day and the quality of sleep they experienced at night. Several patterns emerged. Young adults who had a daily routine—going to work and getting off at the same time each day, eating dinner at the same time, etc.—usually slept better and woke up fewer times during the night than young adults who had a varied routine without a repetitive schedule.

By contrast, older adults in the study sample, if they had inconsistent daily routines, sometimes had better sleep than older adults with consistent schedules. The reason for that may be the amount of stimulation they experienced during the day. Apparently, the more these older adults were active the better chance they had of getting a good night of sleep. This was much truer for older adults than the younger persons. But as Natalie Dautovich, a psychologist at the University of Alabama who led the study research team, noted: "For the majority of sleep outcomes, we found that completing activities at a regular time better predicted sleep outcomes than the actual time of day that activities were completed. For example, people reported better sleep quality and fewer awakenings at night when they were consistent in the time they first went outside" to begin their day.

You should calm yourself before bedtime.

Easing your transition into a state of drowsiness and sleep is important so be careful about the activities you engage in before attempting to sleep. Don't allow yourself to be over-stimulated before bedtime. That could mean don't watch scary or violent movies before trying to sleep, and don't be focused on paying your bills or the concerns and stresses of the day before sleep.

You should also try to avoid any exposure to bright lights just before bedtime. Also, stay clear of your personal workspace, whether it's a home office or a shop in the garage, in the hour or so before getting into bed.

One good way to relax and calm yourself before sleep is to take a long hot shower, or soak in a long hot bath and try a meditation or reciting a mantra as you bask in the soothing water.

You can regulate your sleep routine.

If you are still feeling worked up and agitated before trying to sleep, try out some techniques for stress ventilation. You can do that by expressing your feeling, calmly, to your spouse or another person; you can also write about what you are feeling at the time. However you choose to do it, releasing these feelings before you get into bed helps to calm your mind, which is a necessary ingredient for sleep.

You should monitor your sleep positions.

It may not have occurred to you that your sleep positions affect your sleep quality and sleep duration. Sleep positions are mostly something we take for granted, as if it's mostly beyond our control what positions we take once we fall asleep. This is where some self-examination might be in order.

When you find yourself awake after being interrupted by pain or noises or whatever, what position are you usually in? If there is a pattern you detect (for example, you wake up on your back), it might be worth practicing a visualization as you drift off to sleep, such as imagining yourself never sleeping on your back. When you wake up during the course of the night and you are on your back, make a conscious effort to slip onto your stomach or either side of your body. This ritual can become habitual over time.

If you have gastro esophageal disease, acid reflux problems, or snoring problems or emphysema, try to start off sleeping on the left side of your body and practice staying in that position. Experts say that your right lung is more capable of efficient breathing in that sleeping position than is your left lung.

As indicated earlier in this section of the book, avoid sleeping on your back if you experience chronic snoring. Another body position tip, especially if you have arthritis or experience numbness and tingling in your hands and arms, a consequence of poor circulation, is to consciously keep your arms and hands from being above your head while in bed.

You should restrict your bed to sleeping.

Doing work-related activities of any sort while lying in bed using your laptop or iPad may be a habit that undermines your sleep. It's as if you are programming your thoughts to automatically reflect on challenges and problems in your life each time you climb into your bed zone.

So restrict what you do in bed to sleep and lovemaking. (More on lovemaking will come later in this chapter but, suffice it to say, sex is an exception to this bed distraction guideline for obvious and not so obvious reasons—orgasms release hormones that enable you to relax with sounder and longer sleep.)

You should limit what you consume before bedtime.

It's common sense that eating too much or drinking too much before you attempt to fall asleep can be a recipe for insomnia or interrupted sleep. You probably already know this all too well from experience.

The more you stimulate your digestive tract before laying down the less likely you are to sleep soundly. The same holds true with your consumption of liquids. It's not just the sleep interruption that comes from needing to urinate during the night, it's what might be in those liquids which keeps you awake. Caffeinated drinks are typical culprits, but that glass of wine you have to relax yourself before bed also can play a role in affecting your quality of sleep. Keep in mind that anything you drink containing any amount of caffeine can remain in your system for several hours and that means your body continues to be stimulated until the last traces of caffeine are gone.

You should exercise before dark.

If you do any sort of vigorous exercise just before bedtime you raise your body temperature, which will have an effect similar to caffeine on your system.

Sleep experts advise that you finish your physical exercise at least three hours before turning in for the night. The aftermath of exercise can be relaxing as you burn off the tensions of your day. You just need to get your body temperature down to achieve the deeper relaxation which is a sleep aid.

You can keep a sleep diary.

Dream diaries are for keeping track of your dreams, whereas sleep diaries are for keeping track of your sleeping patterns. Both are designed to give you insights into thoughts and behaviors you may not be consciously aware of.

Such a sleep journal or diary should record the time you got into bed each evening, the frequency of awakening during the night, what you consumed before going to bed, how relaxed (or not) you felt on awakening, and any other sleep related details that might show your overall experience with sleep. Should your problem with getting sufficient sleep continue after trying out the techniques in this book, this sleep journal could prove beneficial to a physician or sleep specialist should you decide to seek professional assistance in your sleep quest.

18 Natural Sleep Enhancers

What you will find below is a possible roadmap of natural techniques and natural substances all of which, together and separately, might benefit you on your journey to wellness and a more satisfying sleep experience.

Consider these to be ideas designed to guide you for your own further research and discovery. Some will require assistance from instructors or therapists, while others you can undertake without any need for outside help.

The important thing to remember is that you are trying out these suggestions to see what works best for you as an individual. There is no 'one-size-fits-all' or 'magic bullet' answer to the question of what brings anyone an effective remedy for sleeplessness any more than there is for relieving pain. Much of what you will find below about sleep remedies also work as pain reducers.

It should be noted that one emerging sleep remedy deserves mention even though the science showing its sleep benefits remains preliminary. Medical marijuana is used by some people with chronic pain to help induce sleep. Other people get their minds so wired up and working overtime after consuming pot that it's detrimental to getting a good night's sleep. A 2011 review of all research studies to that date documenting the effects of cannabis found "several which reported significant improvements in sleep." November 2011, *British Journal of Clinical Pharmacology.*

Acupuncture/Acupressure

What is it? This ancient Chinese practice has achieved widespread acceptance among Western medical practitioners, including the U.S. National Institutes of Health, for its ability to relieve the symptoms of a wide range of ailments, including pain. The application of tiny, thin needles at strategic areas of the body is also used on occasion to treat symptoms of insomnia. As you may have already read or heard, this system is based on the idea that the human body contains a meridian of energy, or pressure spots, which can be stimulated to correct imbalances that cause health problems.

How is it done? Typically an acupuncture practitioner will do an examination of you beforehand, looking at the shape and coloration of your tongue, taking your pulse on both arms, noting the smell of your breath, and other indicators which may seem strange to you. Based on this information and a description from you of your symptoms, a decision will be made as to where the small needles will penetrate your skin. Sometimes the needles are attached to a device that generates small electrical pulses into the body. Your entire session might last for just 10 minutes or up to an hour depending on the practitioner's diagnosis.

If you decide to undergo acupressure instead of using needles, much of the procedure is the same except that the practitioner uses hand or elbow pressure on the meridian points to obtain the desired result.

What is the evidence for it? Skeptics of acupuncture like to say that any perceived benefits come from either the needles activating the brain's release of opioids, or from the patient's own expectations known as the placebo effect. However relief from insomnia comes, let's examine some of the medical study evidence for the benefits available to you.

In a November 2009 study appearing in *The Journal of Alternative and Complementary Medicine*, a team of four physicians looked at how insomnia is treated by acupuncture in China. They examined 46 different published scientific experiments conducted on more than 3,800 people and compared the results. They concluded from this large body of evidence, studies conducted not just in China but all over the world, that "acupuncture appears to be effective in treatment of insomnia."

These four scientists and study authors also noted how acupuncture was shown to be "superior to medications" (which is to say, prescription sleep drugs) in lengthening sleep duration by up to three hours. Not only that, there were no documented side effects from the use of acupuncture, whereas the sleep medications all had some side effects that any health conscious person should have concerns about.

As for the needleless acupressure approach, a study from August 1999 in *The Journal of Gerontology and Biological Science* gives us a compelling piece of important evidence showing the benefits of this technique for insomnia, particularly for our senior citizens. Four scientists did an experiment using acupressure with 84 senior citizens who had diagnosed sleep disturbance conditions. The results were conclusive: "This study confirmed the effectiveness of acupressure in improving the quality of sleep of elderly people and offered a non-pharmacological therapy method for sleep-disturbed elderly people."

Autogenic Training

What is it? Your nervous system has what is called an 'autonomic' component that automatically controls your heartbeat, blood pressure, muscle tension, digestion, and other involuntary functions of your body. This section of your nervous system hosts two parts: sympathetic, called your 'fight or flight' response; and parasympathetic, called your 'rest and digest' response.

This technique called Autogenic Training was created in 1932 to help patients *consciously* balance their sympathetic and parasympathetic systems. That was intended to create a state of whole-body relaxation in order to calm your heart, lower your blood pressure, and rejuvenate your immune system. This might be potentially quite useful for insomniacs and folks whose pain keeps them from getting uninterrupted sleep.

How to do it? A session of this training, according to therapists who used it with clients, might consist of the following general steps: (1) You sit in a meditative posture quietly, eyes closed, and mentally visualize your body. (2) You start this visualization with your arms and slowly repeat three times, "my arms are heavy and warm." (3) Then you do the same procedure with your legs, and repeat three times, "my arms and legs are heavy and warm." (4) Finally, repeat three times as you visualize your heart and say, "my heartbeat is calm and regular."

Once your entire body is relaxed, try putting the focus of all of your attention on a needy area—a sore muscle or an area of your body where you feel pain. It might be most helpful to use this technique just before bedtime.

What is the evidence for it? Three scientists in Britain writing in the journal *Primary Health Care Research* published their study in April 2012 which used 153 sleep disorder patients to test whether Autogenic Training was an effective alternative to drugs for insomnia. After eight weeks those who underwent the training were reporting a quicker onset of sleep, falling asleep faster after waking during the night, feeling more rested upon waking, and less anxiety and depression during the day. Concluded the study: "Autogenic Training may improve sleep patterns for patients with various health conditions and reduce anxiety and depression, both of which may result from and cause insomnia. Improvements in sleep patterns occurred despite, or possibly due to, not focusing on sleep during training. Autogenic Training may provide an approach to insomnia that could be incorporated into primary care."

Biofeedback

What is it? Suppose you could diminish or eliminate pain and sleeplessness simply by placing the focus of your attention on the area of pain or on the impediments to your good sleep, and then activate your mind to remedy the problem? Wouldn't you be inclined to try out this approach to see if it works for you?

Many people who use the various biofeedback techniques claim they can accomplish this mind-over-matter effect because biofeedback enables you to measure your bodily processes and conveys that information to you in real time. As your awareness of your body is raised, you begin to gain conscious control over some physiological activities that are normally automatic. A biofeedback machine monitors everything from your skin temperature to your heart rate. By seeing the readings simultaneously as you feel the sensations, you learn to mentally control both the readings and the sensations until you can accomplish this without being hooked to any biofeedback device.

When you use temperature biofeedback, for instance, it can help you to treat some circulatory disorders and reduce the frequency of migraine headaches. Among other conditions successfully treated with biofeedback training has been incontinence, chronic indigestion, Attention Deficit Hyperactivity Disorder, backaches, neck pain, fibromyalgia, the rehabilitation of motor skills in stroke victims and in people suffering from multiple sclerosis, and in the treatment of Parkinson's disease symptoms.

If you consult the experts associated with the Association for Applied Psychophysiology and Biofeedback, which you can find on the Internet, the steps involved in mastering this at-home technique are presented. It will first involve having a session with a biofeedback technician, then learning to monitor the physical sensations on your own. These experts will also describe how to use biofeedback along with self-hypnosis to evoke the placebo response in a way that creates a powerful synergy for you to harness in dealing with pain and insomnia.

What is the evidence for it? In the 1997 American Psychological Association book, *Understanding Sleep: The Evaluation and Treatment of Sleep Disorders*, a chapter was included which summarized the study evidence for biofeedback and other behavioral techniques as treatments for insomnia. Three types of biofeedback were described as being "effective in studies" for treating insomnia and sleep problems in general.

1. **EMG (electromyography)**: In this relaxation procedure, patients receive biofeedback-assisted relaxation training on a biofeedback machine from an expert, and then they are taught a relaxation procedure they can use at home when biofeedback machines are unavailable. "The EMG biofeedback literature suggests that this can be an effective treatment for insomnia," noted the psychology guidebook.

2. **EEG (theta electroencephalography)**: In this biofeedback device the attempt is made to induce sleep directly by stimulating the productions of theta waves in the brain and stage one sleep. Some research has indicated theta biofeedback can bring about faster sleep induction than other types of relaxation training.

3. **SMR EEG (sensorimotor electroencephalography)**: In this technique the biofeedback machine is used to strengthen brain wave rhythm from the sensorimotor cortex region of the brain, which is thought to coincide with the brain waves that induce deepening sleep. Studies have shown this method brought on sleep faster and reduced the number of body movements during sleep, thus increasing the time spent in the REM sleep stage.

Research comparing the results of these three biofeedback procedures found that people who were most tense benefitted the most from EMG biofeedback. By contrast, those patients who were the least tense before undergoing the procedure got the most sleep benefit from SMR biofeedback.

Cognitive Behavioral Therapy

What is it? It can help you sleep, ease anxiety, and deal with cancer pain. This technique called cognitive therapy has as its first step showing you how to identify the *thoughts* that lead you down the dark paths of negativity, such as *catastrophe thinking,* in which your mind always turns to expecting the worst to happen, and the thought process of *minimizing*, in which you downplay everything that can be said to be good about you. The next step is that you learn how to substitute much more realistic, practical, and positive thoughts so you are less likely to engage in self-sabotage.

Your thoughts can either enhance or obstruct your ability to heal from pain or to overcome insomnia, but you can change your thoughts and their underlying toxic beliefs so that your mind can improve your health. That's the basic idea behind cognitive behavior therapy.

One of the best and most documented approaches to CBT was developed by experts at the University of Pennsylvania School of Medicine, where this technique was invented specifically for using the mind to aid in healing. If you do an Internet search under the terms 'Cognitive Therapy' or 'Cognitive Behavioral Therapy' you will be able to find a therapist using the technique in your area for your specific problem, and you will learn how to implement and benefit from a short term treatment using CBT. Medical experts at Mayo Clinic have shown how anyone can break the pattern of repetitive negative thoughts and the belief system that generates them.

Doing a series of simple steps overseen by a qualified therapist can help you to create an action plan for behavioral changes, enabling you to write new mental scripts to navigate the health challenges, particularly pain and insomnia, and the other difficulties encountered in life.

What is the evidence for it? Cognitive therapy is designed to reverse any one or all of the five states of mind contributing to insomnia symptoms: 1) worry 2) attention distractions 3) negative beliefs about sleep 4) inability to accurately gauge the impact of sleep deficits on daytime performance 5) other behaviors that reinforce unhelpful beliefs about sleep. The act of using cognitive therapy to change these negative attitudes and beliefs is called cognitive restructuring.

Many studies have been done to assess how effective cognitive therapy can be in treating insomnia and sleep impairment. In a 2007 study in *Behavioral Research Therapy*, for instance, 19 patients with serious insomnia issues were treated with cognitive therapy and then monitored over 12 months at the Sleep and Psychological Disorders lab at the University of California at Berkeley. The study authors concluded: "The significant improvement in both nighttime and daytime impairment evidence at the post treatment assessment was retained up to the 12-month follow-up."

Still another important study, this one published in an April 2001 issue of the *Journal of the American Medical Association*, a team of researchers described their remarkable results obtained from using cognitive behavioral therapy on 75 adults (with an average age 55 years old) who had lived with insomnia symptoms for 13 years or more. "Our results suggest that cognitive behavioral treatment represents a viable intervention for primary sleep-maintenance insomnia," the five scientists wrote. "This treatment leads to clinically significant sleep improvements within six weeks and these improvements appear to endure through six months of follow-up."

Foods

What is it? You know the answer to this one. It's what you eat, but not everything you eat. Not all foods were created equal when it comes to influencing your ability to sleep well. What you eat can either help you to induce sleep, or certain other foods will sabotage your sleep.

Some of the best research I have seen on the connections between your foods, dietary habits, and relieving pain while enhancing your ability to sleep has come from Dr. Neal Barnard, president of the Physicians' Committee for Responsible Medicine.

First, here are the three foods that are the most common sleep saboteurs.

- ✔ Pizza, tomato sauce, and spicy foods are the culprits most likely to cause heartburn, acid reflux, and other disturbances of your gastric system which can, in turn, interrupt or delay restful sleep.

- ✔ Chocolate contains caffeine and tyrosine, a stimulating amino acid. Eating this before bedtime may end up keeping your mind and body stimulated when you want to be relaxed.

- ✔ Smoked and preserved meats contain the amino acid tyramine, a chemical that triggers your brain to release norepinephrine; it is this latter chemical which acts as a stimulant for alertness and your body will experience it in high concentrations from consuming smoked meats, ham, bacon, and sausage. These should be considered off limits before going to bed.

You should also probably avoid any high protein foods in the evening since they can undermine your body's production of serotonin, a neurotransmitter that is a natural sleep enhancer and pain reliever.

Sugar can help you to fall asleep, reports Dr. Barnard (just don't take your sugar in the form of chocolate). Sugar helps your brain to stimulate the production of serotonin. Since sugar should be avoided in large quantities due to its role in producing weight gain, it's best to use a small amount of a fruit sugar, such as orange juice, rather than a tablespoon of white or brown sugar.

Just about every media outlet, from the BBC to *Woman's Day* and *Reader's Digest*, even the business magazine *Forbes*, has weighed in with their experts on which foods best promote sleep. Here are some of the consensus favorites, most of which stimulate your production of tryptophan and serotonin, the sleepy hormones. Others contain and then stimulate melatonin in your body, which is found in much higher levels in plants than in animals, another good reason for us to eat a primarily plant-based diet.

A bowl of grain cereal is a big favorite, or even a bowl of oatmeal. Bananas also contain tryptophan and eating one before sleeping might help you to relax. Miso soup contains amino acids that also boost your body's serotonin supply, so try a warm bowl of instant miso an hour or so before going to bed. Believe it or not, according to WebMD, chicken contains more tryptophan than turkey, despite what you may think you feel after every Thanksgiving dinner. Hummus is another good source for tryptophan, and so are dates.

Nutrition researchers at the University of Rochester found that a glass of cherry juice, especially when made with tart cherries, boosts your body's production of melatonin, which is the best natural sleep aid. You can also try eating a handful of dried tart cherries about an hour before bedtime. A study published in 2012 in *The European Journal of Nutrition* recommended drinking two glasses of tart cherry juice a day to get the best results in achieving longer and more restful sleep.

Guided Imagery

What is it? There is quite a bit of evidence from medical science studies showing the benefits of using a sequence of soothing images before bedtime to quiet your mind and relax your body for rest.

Maybe you already have had experience with its effects and didn't realize it. A good example is if you've had the experience of daydreaming at work and the daydream is so vivid and real that you can actually feel yourself experiencing a different place than where you are.

At the Academy for Guided Imagery, neuroscientists teach how to use guided imagery to lessen your illness symptoms and to enhance your immune system functioning. This practical, low-cost and easy to use tool has proven effective for lots of self-care, particularly among cancer patients. A review by the American Cancer Society of 46 studies on imagery and cancer revealed that it was effective for reducing pain, stress, depression, and other side effects associated with cancer treatment. Dr. Carl Simonton has even demonstrated its effectiveness in killing cancer cells by visualizing their shrinkage.

Some of the best results with imagery have come in treating the toughest patients—people with chronic insomnia, or who suffer from chronic nightmares due to posttraumatic stress disorders (PTSD). Children with nightmares have also obtained proven benefits. It has a lot of relief-giving potential.

Imagery rehearsal therapy is the term that sleep experts use to describe this approach to inducing relaxation that leads to slumber. It is done prior to bedtime and it provides a transition for you to enter stage one sleep.

What is the evidence for it? Here are a few of the many studies showing that sleep imagery can be effective if you will take the time to try it out:

Several Oxford University (UK) psychologists gave 41 people with insomnia one of three instructional sets to follow before attempting to fall asleep. Imagery 'distraction' was one of those three programs and it proved its worth in practice, enabling the test subjects to fall asleep faster. As the researchers reported in a March 2002 issue of the British journal, *Behaviour Research and Therapy,* "the success of the imagery distraction task is attributed to it occupying sufficient 'cognitive space' to keep the individual from re-engaging with thoughts, worries, and concerns during the pre-sleep period."

Writing in a 2006 issue of the U.S. journal *Behavior Sleep Medicine,* two researchers with the Sleep & Human Health Institute of New Mexico reported that of all the treatments proposed for chronic nightmares, a sleep disorder experienced by up to 8% of the general population, "imagery rehearsal therapy has received the most empirical support."

A large team of researchers from the Sleep & Human Health Institute did a major investigation of 168 women who experienced chronic nightmares and other sleep disturbances as a result of sexual assault and posttraumatic stress. Their findings, reported in an August 2001 issue of the *Journal of the American Medical Association,* determined that "imagery rehearsal therapy is a well-tolerated treatment that appears to decrease chronic nightmares, improve sleep quality, and decrease posttraumatic stress disorder symptom severity."

Homeopathy

What is it? By taking small quantities of substances from nature, which have been used over hundreds of years by various cultures worldwide, homeopathic practitioners create treatments for many ailments, including sleep problems. The idea is that miniscule amounts of a plant or mineral can trigger the self-healing mechanisms of the human body. Mainstream medicine absolutely abhors homeopathy claiming that it is the placebo effect, and it is widely controversial (but when have I ever shied away from controversy!?).

How do you use it? Dr. James Forsythe, a pioneering Nevada oncologist and homeopathic physician, has compiled a list of some of the substances that he most commonly recommends to his patients as sleep inducers. His recommendations are based on long-term trial and error testing. Among them:

- ✔ **Arsenicum album**: Sold in tablet, liquid or powder form, it is made by baking a combination of minerals and is prescribed for insomnia and anxiety.

- ✔ **Cocculus**: Known as 'moonseed', it's a substance found in tropical climates and is often recommended for people who say they are too tired to sleep.

- ✔ **Ignatia amara**: A pear-shaped fruit from China and the Philippines, its derivatives are another treatment for insomnia.

- ✔ **Lycopodium**: Called 'Wolfpaw clubmoss', it's another natural sleep aid.

- ✔ **Nux vomica**: From a Southeast Asian tree called evergreen strychnine, it's used for insomnia.

- ✔ **Silica**: Comes from flint and is used as a sleep enhancer.

✔ **Sulphur**: Found naturally in certain minerals, it's sometimes considered helpful for insomnia caused by not exercising enough.

✔ **Natural Herbs**: These are non-addictive sleep remedies and include valerium and chamomile, passion-flower, and St. John's wort.

What is the evidence for it? Mainstream medicine tells us that homeopathy is nothing more than the placebo effect, our expectations that homeopathic remedies work accounting for whatever success the remedies have. If it is indeed a placebo effect and it still works as effectively as a drug, then why not try it?

A study in the September 2013 issue of *Alternative Therapeutic Health Medicine* described how 46 males between the ages of 18 and 40, all with chronic insomnia, were put through a four-week experiment at the University of Johannesburg, South Africa, that used a homeopathic remedy complex in a 20% alcohol solution. Concluded the study authors: "Findings suggest that daily use of the homeopathic complex does have an effect over a four-week period" in relieving many symptoms associated with insomnia.

German scientists wrote in the February 2013 issue of the *Journal of Alternative and Complementary Medicine* how they tested a homeopathic combination remedy on 40 women aged 30 to 50 years to determine if stress could be lowered to improve sleep quality. Sleep improvement along with better hormonal functioning that promoted sleep was found in most of the study subjects.

Hypnosis

What is it? Just before you fall asleep you enter a slightly hypnotic state. You may also find yourself entering it when you're deeply immersed in a tedious task or in reading a particularly engrossing book. Daydreaming is another way to experience this state of mind which is trancelike.

Most of us enter what can be called trance states numerous times during the daily routine of our lives. Dr. Larry Dossey calls hypnosis a window into the soul of healing, and that statement receives support from hundreds of medical studies showing how hypnotic states and self-hypnosis can alleviate health symptoms and even help to cure some types of health maladies. Here are just a few examples of these peer-reviewed and randomized controlled medical studies:

✔ Hypnosis accelerates the healing of bone fractures and reduces the pain associated with broken bones and cuts down on the need for medications.

✔ Self-hypnosis reduces anxiety after coronary bypass surgery and facilitates faster healing and a reduction in medication requirements.

✔ Burn wound healing undergoes "dramatic enhancement" when hypnosis is used. What made this study, published in the *American Journal of Clinical Hypnosis,* even more remarkable was that patients were told during hypnosis that only one part of their burned body would heal faster—and it did!

Hypnosis specialists, like psychologist Dr. Rick Levy, use the practice in their private sessions with patients who have health challenges. If you do an Internet search under the terms 'hypnosis' and 'self-hypnosis' and 'hypnosis and sleep' you will find information to take you through the steps necessary to develop your own self-hypnosis program that can be tailored to your specific health concerns or sleep-related problems.

What is the evidence for it? The use of hypnotherapy to manage various types of sleep disorders has been studied by groups of scientists throughout the world. In the Singapore medical journal *Annals of the Academy of Medicine*, for instance, an August 2008 review of the medical literature on hypnosis and sleep disorders found that "acute and chronic insomnia often respond to relaxation and hypnotherapy approaches." The study authors pointed out "there is a major placebo effect" with the use of hypnosis (a sort of mind-over-matter effect), and hypnosis should be used as part of a complete medical treatment package.

At the Northwestern University Feinberg School of Medicine several researchers also did an overview review of the medical literature regarding hypnosis and the management of sleep disorders. Their findings, published in a 2007 issue of the *International Journal of Clinical and Experimental Hypnosis*, made a case that the most effective use of hypnosis and self-hypnosis techniques are to combine them with cognitive behavioral therapy. Once again this study conclusion echoes what I recommend throughout this book—try combining several techniques at once for maximum results to see what works best for you.

Mantras

What is it? Unknowingly, you used a form of mantra if you ever tried 'counting sheep' in order to clear your mind and lull yourself into slumber.

The word 'mantra' comes from the ancient Sanskrit of India and means a word grouping that is a sacred utterance. A literal translation from Sanskrit means 'an instrument of thought'. It can be repeated as a prayer, meditation or an incantation. Both Hinduism and Buddhism use mantras, but variations of sacred chants or hymns can be found in Christianity and other religions. The word 'om', for instance, can be used as a mantra when its syllables are stretched out (oooommmm) and then repeated.

Whether they have any meaning for you or not, think of mantras as soothing melodic sounds. Much like some forms of music (think classical) these sounds can help to calm your mind and relax your body, except instead of free flowing like music, mantras get their effects from the rhythmic constant repetition.

If you do a search on the Internet under 'mantras and sleep' you will find numerous examples of mantras some folks use to get restful sleep. (For example, http://www.spiritvoyage.com/blog/index.php/3-mantras-to-help-insomnia/.)

(For a calming word exercise you can use as part of your natural remedy toolbox for inducing sleep, see the Appendix and Script Two offered to you by psychotherapist Donald Altman found later in the book.)

What is the evidence for it? Though scientists don't use the word mantra (they use the term 'articulatory suppression') the process they have in mind is similar to the repetition of mantras using either a single word or phrases. The first major research study laying out how articulatory suppression can treat insomnia came in 1991 with four scientists writing in the journal *Behavioral Research Therapy*. In their procedure, insomnia patients repeated simple words, such as 'the', about three or four times a second, which is rather fast, much faster than mantras are normally repeated. This technique has since been used as an insomnia treatment to reduce the interference of recurrent thoughts that disrupt sleep. It has been considered to be an effective self-help approach with results which have been replicated in laboratory settings.

Meditation

What is it? To clear your mind and experience the 'power of now', you don't need to be a yogi master or a believer in an Eastern religion. Meditation can be part of a spiritual practice, but it is also a safe and simple technique to enhance your health and overall well-being, to bring about faster healing after illness or injury, and to put you in a state of mind to make restful sleep more possible.

Meditation practices are being prescribed and successfully used for such conditions as anxiety, stress, skin diseases, infertility, chronic pain, high blood pressure, insulin levels, heart attack and stroke prevention, immune system stimulation, obsessive-compulsive disorder, depression, and other psychiatric conditions. Because meditation helps to relax both the body and mind, it is a natural and effective approach for your self-treatment of sleep problems.

By slowing your breath and quieting your mind, you can bring about deep relaxation and learn to tap into your body's own inner healing wisdom. Though numerous meditation techniques exist—such as Vipassana, Kriya, and Transcendental Meditation—many medical researchers, like University of Wisconsin neuroscientist Richard Davidson, use combinations or variations on all of the techniques. (Once again, we have touched on a theme of this book—try out combinations of remedies for best results.)

How to do it? The general steps of how to go about meditating and integrating that practice into your life are quite simple. As with any relaxation technique, you need a quite place where you won't be interrupted by other people, ringing telephones, or outside noise.

Begin by sitting straight upright in a chair, relaxing your hands on your thighs. Close your eyes. Start taking slow, deep breaths. Breathe in slowly through your nose, and exhale slowly through your slightly parted lips. As thoughts arise, don't focus on them. Just let the thoughts slip past your awareness as if each thought was a train car passing slowly by on a train track. You watch the train car (your thought) pass by and out of sight. Keep your attention and awareness, as much as possible, focused on your breathing.

With practice, the slow, deep breaths will come more naturally and the thoughts will arise less frequently. Meditate for at least five minutes the first time, then 10 minutes the second time, and lengthen your meditations over time. Obviously, this will take a lot of practice. But it will be worth it.

There are many meditation traditions and techniques for using your breath. You can find more information by doing an Internet search (try the key words 'meditation and sleep') and usually the explanations detailed by experts are easy to understand. You will find YouTube videos online that take you through the steps of using meditation for insomnia. There are many meditation techniques, too many to give examples in these pages.

What is the evidence for it? There is a mixed bag of research results on the effectiveness of meditation in treating insomnia and other sleep disorders. Let's try to sort through it all to give you the best and most up to date possible information.

First, let's share the not-so-good news. Many studies show that a meditation practice 'awakens the mind', which is to say, in the aftermath of doing meditation the mind is aroused with focus and clarity. That mental state can interfere with bringing about the onset of sleep. This was the finding of a July 2010 review of the medical literature in the journal *Psychosomatic Medicine*. It's not that meditation made sleep worse, according to Willoughby Britton, a clinical psychologist at Brown University who co-authored this study, but that meditation just didn't "promote better, deeper sleep."

What did become apparent from the consensus findings of the research was that meditation improved depression, at least among depressed persons who meditated at least 30 minutes per day, and this improvement led to better sleep. The same correlation may exist for pain. As meditation improves the experience of pain, it may lead to an improved quality of sleep. So the benefits of meditation for improved sleep may be indirect instead of direct.

There are some other exceptions worth noting. One impact of sleep deprivation is a decline in your cognitive functions. In other words, your mind isn't as effective when you are sleep deprived and that can hurt you professionally and in your personal relationships. Study findings published in a December 2012 issue of the *Indian Journal of Medical Research* showed how a group of volunteers from the Indian Army were deprived of sleep for 36 hours and then tested before and after doing a meditation practice. Their mental performance was "improved to a significant extent using meditation," the research team reported.

Finally, there is strong evidence that self-relaxation training combining progressive muscle relaxation with meditation practice can improve sleep quality in one particular group of people— senior citizens. *The Journal of Clinical Nursing* presented a study in May 2013 that tested 80 senior citizens using this combination of muscle relaxation and meditation. The results were quite encouraging and should be good news for anyone over the age of 60 years. Concluded the study authors: "Self-relaxation training is a non-invasive, simple, and inexpensive therapeutic method of improving sleep quality and cognitive functions in community-dwelling older people."

Melatonin

What is it? If you've tried prescription sleeping pills, you probably know they may knock you out, but they don't provide you with the restful stage four delta sleep that your mind and body needs. One natural alternative that can provide you with delta sleep stage is melatonin. It's a substance that regulates the body's circadian rhythm, the daily 24-hour cycle that oversees vital functions. The pineal gland at the center of the brain produces this vital substance.

Surrounded by a rich blood supply, the pineal gland contains 100 times more serotonin than any part of the human body. Serotonin acts as a kind of thermostat system in the body, relaying and amplifying signals between neurons and other cells. Serotonin serves as an important precursor or direct parent of melatonin.

Melatonin also regulates production of the stress-regulator cortisol and the sex hormone testosterone, which manages energy, libido, and red blood cell production—while also protecting the body against osteoporosis.

Your body's production of melatonin decreases as you age, peaking from ages 15 to 25, before decreasing to 15 to 20 percent of those levels by the time you reach 70 years of age and more.

Because serotonin levels remain high in people of advanced age, the balance between melatonin and serotonin weighs in favor of serotonin as we get older. Negative symptoms can emerge from this imbalance, most notably interrupted sleep patterns, central sleep apnea, sexual dysfunction, depression, and a tendency to develop Type 2 diabetes mellitus.

The eventual dominance of serotonin in mature people emerges as a harmful development, largely because melatonin plays a vital role in enhancing the essential sleep process, which is important to your body's healing.

Clinical results consistently show how this hormone battles free radicals hidden in toxic substances absorbed from food, water, and the environment, toxins that can contribute to the aging process.

What is the evidence for it? Melatonin also defends brain function by warding off free radicals. It may also decrease heart disease and immune deficiency diseases. In a study at the University of Texas Health Center in San Antonio, rats given carcinogens before melatonin treatments had 50 percent less genetic damage than those without such therapy. Melatonin is a proven immune system booster and offers relief to people suffering from chronic depression.

Keep in mind that melatonin isn't just important for getting restful sleep. It has numerous other well documented advantages and one of them may be to extend lifespans. Physicians have found that middle-aged and older people who have never taken melatonin supplements experience decreased quality and duration of sleep. Their immune system functions, their vitality and longevity diminish as well.

Due to the pineal gland's strategic location within the brain, the body secretes melatonin directly into the cerebrospinal fluid and the general circulatory system. Our bodies drastically reduce the production of melatonin during daylight hours, following its usual peak at about three in the morning.

Medical professionals say that melatonin acts as the body's biological clock due to the hormone's relationship to light and dark cycles. Seasonal changes impact this process, when daylight hours expand during summers and shorten during winters.

People older than 50 who use melatonin supplements should start these regimens by taking lower doses, such as 1 to 3 milligrams at bedtime. This process usually entails taking melatonin every other day or a maximum five to six days per week.

Be sure to avoid taking melatonin at least one day per week in order to allow the pineal gland to continue making this hormone uninhibited.

After initial regimens have progressed for a while, some individuals can easily tolerate nightly bedtime melatonin doses of 10 to 30 milligrams. But it's important for pregnant or nursing mothers, or women trying to conceive, to avoid taking over-the-counter melatonin.

Physicians have been unable to find or develop an effective prescription drug to treat the condition known as sleep apnea. Yet, melatonin in higher doses, as much as 10 or 20 milligrams taken before bedtime, may lessen the negative effects of sleep apnea in some people.

Somnapure is a new product containing herbal ingredients such as chamomile and passion-flower, which are said to have a calming effect on the body. The formula also contains melatonin. This supplement is advertised as being gentle but effective in helping you to get back into a healthy sleeping routine.

Mindfulness

What is it? It's been said that the state of mindfulness is like standing on a metaphorical subway platform and clearly and calmly observing each 'car' of the subway train as it passes by—each thought, opinion, sensation, and emotion—*without* jumping on that subway train and riding it down the track.

Think of mindfulness as a moment-to-moment attentiveness where you pay attention to your thoughts, your feelings, your sensations, your perceptions, your opinions, your memories; whatever may be happening in your life, you do the mindfulness without judgment or rejection or blaming anyone. In many ways it's the opposite of stress, you know, that worried, unsettled, past- and future-fixated state of mind that releases the hormones that undermine good health, like cortisol and adrenalin.

How to do it? Being able to harness our mental awareness to reduce stress and fight illness and disease was an idea that was brought into the medical mainstream in our country by Jon

Kabat-Zinn, a Professor of Medicine emeritus at the University of Massachusetts. He is also the founding executive director of the Center for Mindfulness in Medicine, Health Care, and Society.

Dr. Kabat-Zinn describes how there are two ways to bring mindfulness into your life:

Try mastering it through a formal meditation practice, carving out time each day to be alone, and then to drop into an inward silence and stillness. You can learn to enter and dwell in deep states of relaxation and well-being.

You can also practice it by remembering to bring a spacious, moment-to-moment, non-judgmental awareness to every situation you find yourself in during your day. This is called *informal* mindfulness practice—and it's much easier to do this when you are also practicing formally on a regular basis.

"The most important thing to remember about mindfulness meditation is that it is about paying attention non-judgmentally in the present moment," says Dr. Kabat-Zinn. "We emphasize the present moment because that is the only time any of us are alive. The past is over, the future hasn't happened yet, and the only way we can effectively influence the future is by living fully and consciously in the moments in which we are actually alive, which is always NOW."

Seven keys or states of mind combine to enhance the effects of mindfulness on your body's ability to regenerate itself. Here they are from Kabat-Zinn:

✔ **Be Non-Judging** — Become an impartial witness to inner and outer experiences that we might otherwise be reactive to.

✔ **Practice Patience** — Allow yourself to watch events unfold without the stress and anxiety that comes from rushing everything.

✔ **Have a Beginner's Mind** — By dropping your belief about how things 'should' be, you experience events and people in your life as if for the first time.

✔ **Exercise Trust** — When you don't trust your feelings, or discount them because of peer pressure, you sabotage a powerful tool in the arsenal of self-healing.

✔ **Focus on Non-Striving** — When you try to will yourself to relax, the result can be more stress. It's better to release the striving for results, moment by moment.

✔ **Turn To Acceptance** — If you expend energy trying to resist what already is in the present, you lose the opportunity to be fully present.

✔ **Learning When To Let Go** — The mind tends to cling to certain thoughts, feelings, and situations, both positive and negative. In mindfulness it's important to put aside this tendency to elevate certain experiences while rejecting others as unimportant.

To try a mindfulness meditation technique, assume a comfortable posture lying on your back or sitting. If you're sitting, keep your spine straight and let your shoulders drop. Close your eyes.

"The easiest and most effective way to begin practicing mindfulness as a formal meditation practice is to simply focus your attention on your breathing and see what happens as you attempt to keep it there," says Dr. Kabat-Zinn.

You will find many different places in the body where your breath can be observed. Start with the nostrils—focus on the feeling of the breath as it flows past the nostrils. Another place to observe is your chest as it expands and contracts. Another is your belly, moving it in and out with each breath.

Stay aware of the sensations that accompany your breathing at the particular place where your attention is focused and hold them in the forefront of your awareness from moment to moment. Feel the air as it flows in and out past the nostrils. Feel the movement of the muscles associated with breathing. Feel your stomach as it moves in and out and up and down.

Remember that when you pay attention to your breathing, just do that and nothing more. Don't push or force your breath, or try to make it deeper, or change its rhythm. Resist the need to control it. Remain aware of the *feeling* of each breath in, and each breath out.

If you notice that your mind has wondered away from your breath, make passing note of what took you away and then gently bring your attention back to the feeling of the breath.

Try practicing this exercise for fifteen minutes at a convenient time every day. Do this for one week. This is enough time for you to feel what it's like to incorporate a meditation practice into your routine.

Stay aware of how it feels to spend some time each day just being with your breath without feeling compelled to do or say anything.

What is the evidence for it? Studies show that a mindfulness technique called Mindfulness-Based Stress Reduction can reduce the burden of many different diseases and health conditions, including pain and sleep-related issues. It works by relieving the underlying stress that plays a role in the onset of these health issues and intensifies the symptoms once they appear.

We know that sleep disturbances can compromise your health and the twins 'worry' and 'stress' often cause or intensify these disturbances. To examine the extent to which a course in mindfulness meditation can relieve those symptoms and bring about more restful sleep, a study published in the journal *Explore*, done by researchers from the Department of Family Medicine and Community Health, University of Minnesota, reviewed 38 medical study articles published in medical journals testing the impact of mindfulness practices on sleep habits.

Here is what the study concluded: "There is some evidence to suggest that increased practice of mindfulness techniques is associated with improved sleep and that mindfulness participants experience a decrease in sleep-interfering cognitive processes."

Elsewhere in this book I have urged you to try many of these natural approaches to treating pain and insomnia by combining the techniques to experiment with what works best for you and your unique conditions. Here we have another opportunity to do that.

More researchers writing in the journal *Explore*, this time in January 2009, described how they combined mindfulness mediation and cognitive behavioral therapy to treat insomnia in 21 patients with diagnosed sleep-related problems. These folks were monitored for 12 months as the study participants monitored their own progress using sleep and meditation diaries, and questionnaires related to their sleep habits and sleep-related distress. Numerous benefits for achieving restful sleep were observed and maintained over the year of observation. Combining the two natural treatment approaches had magnified the positive results.

Orgasms

What is it? No need for me to tell you what an orgasm is unless you are one of the unfortunate few who has never experienced one. It's easy to overlook how one natural bodily function—your sexuality—can enhance your experience of another natural bodily function—restful sleep.

Both men and women experience a drop in blood pressure after having an orgasm, though this process occurs faster in men. This may be one reason for the widely held perception that men fall asleep quickly after sex while women usually want to cuddle and may even act frisky again.

A blood pressure drop after orgasm is accompanied by the release of endorphin hormones and these provide an effective tranquilizer for many people who have trouble falling asleep.

There are several other benefits from orgasms which indirectly provide relief from sleep problems.

You reduce your stress levels. Nothing quite wipes away tensions of the day as the release that comes from lovemaking. You will certainly sleep better afterwards, and the more this becomes a ritual or routine in your life, the less accumulation of stress you will feel in your body.

You can relieve depression. Hormones such as the endorphins that you release after orgasm are guaranteed mood elevators. Minor and short term depression can be lifted and this will enhance your sleep. If the depression is severe or long term, then sexual intimacy will often be thwarted by impotence and lack of desire, resulting in sleep loss. So if you suffer from severe depression, seek professional care, the faster the better.

You can relieve minor pains. Pain is a sleep disturber, even when minor in nature. Orgasms release oxytocin, a natural pain reliever, into your body along with other natural opiates. These combine to create an analgesic effect which you may find helpful in reducing pain associated with arthritis and other ailments.

What is the evidence for it? Your frequency of orgasms has been shown in medical studies to be directly related to living longer. On average, people who have two or more orgasms a week have half the death rate of similarly aged people who give themselves orgasms just once a month. Part of the reason may be that sexually satisfied people sleep longer and experience a higher quality of sleep than people who habitually deny themselves this natural pleasure of life.

You've probably also heard or, if you're a male, even experienced, how drowsiness comes over men after ejaculation. It's an effect from the slew of hormones and neurotransmitters that are released with orgasm. So to get the maximum amount of sleep benefit from sex, time your orgasms to just before you want to enter sleep.

Relaxation Response

What is it? You don't always know when stress is stalking you. It can creep up on you over time, a shadow that grows larger until it brazenly overpowers your mind and body like a mugger in broad daylight. Your immune system falls prey first, rendering you vulnerable. Insomnia is often a byproduct of stress that is out of control.

Stress is the number one trigger for illness and disease. The Relaxation Response is a self-help therapeutic technique which can help. It involves repeating a word, sound, prayer or other phrases (much like a mantra) as you sit quietly in a comfortable position, your eyes closed, as you breathe slowly, relaxing each part of your body. You do this for 10 to 20 minutes twice a day. You can also use visual imagery to heighten this relaxation effect.

Harvard Medical School Professor Herbert Benson, founder of the Mind/Body Medical Institute, created the Relaxation Response four decades ago. It's a deceptively powerful yet simple way to strengthen your immune system or to treat many stress-connected disorders and diseases. When activated, your metabolism slows, as do your heartbeat and breathing, and your muscles relax, and the levels of nitric oxide in your body increase.

What is the evidence for it? Among the range of health maladies that studies indicate can be treated with this technique are: Alcoholism, Anxiety, Auto-Immune Disorders, Burns, Headaches, Insomnia, Multiple Sclerosis, Nausea, Neurodegenerative Diseases, Pain, Stress, Tooth Extraction.

A review of the results from several hundred studies examining the relaxation response, done in a 2001 issue of the *Journal of Alternative and Complementary Medicine*, found that headaches and insomnia were two of the more effective treatments for which the technique can be used.

Tai Chi

What is it? It began in China and remains popular there, which is why you may have seen photos or videos showing groups of people, quite often elderly Chinese, standing together outdoors in parks, and moving slowly and rhythmically as if they were taking a martial arts class. This moving meditation called Tai Chi is a 'soft' martial arts technique. It is intended for the practitioner to use their mind to train their body for health enhancement.

You don't need to become a Tai Chi expert to receive benefit from the practice. There are many websites which provide useful advice on how to integrate a Tai Chi practice into your life for the best results. Solo routines can be done (you don't always need to be part of a group), and even solo you can pick up the series of movements which can be learned naturally, by placing an emphasis on your coordination while in relaxation. As with the other relaxation techniques described in the pages of this book, Tai Chi is a tool best used in combination with other sleep enhancing suggestions.

What is the evidence for it? In an October 2008 study appearing in the scientific journal *Sleep*, researchers from the David Geffen School of Medicine at UCLA described how they took a group of

112 healthy older adults between the ages of 59 and 86, and taught them 20 Tai Chi moves they practiced over 25 weeks. Sleep quality was the biggest single benefit reported by the test subjects. "They took the least time to fall asleep, had fewer awakenings, and felt better rested," said Dr. Michael Irwin, lead author of the study, in an interview with AARP. "The amount of sleep across the night was longer, and they slept a greater amount of time."

Technology for Sleep

Technology advancement promises a future of 'smarter' and sounder sleep.

What is it? What NASA has learned about sleep induction technology to benefit its astronauts could end up in your bedroom soon to further your quest for developing healthy sleep habits. Sometime in 2016 a light-color-changing system for sleep enhancement will be installed on the International Space Station.

By having the lighting system change colors from blue to yellow or white and then to red throughout scheduled sleep periods, research by NASA indicated that feelings of sleepiness could be induced by the light wavelengths stimulating the release of the hormone melatonin. This could be an important rest innovation for astronauts who never have the benefit of complete darkness for extended periods of time as they orbit the Earth.

At the 2014 Consumer Electronics Show in Las Vegas several different similar sleep technologies were unveiled. The one receiving the most attention was called the Aura Smart Sleep system selling for around $300. This system comes as a collection of smart parts: a soft padded sensor that goes under your mattress to record your breathing cycles, body movements, and heart rate; a device that tucks next to your bed using sensors to monitor changes in your environment, including light levels, noise, and temperature variations; connected to this device is a clock and speaker playing alarm sounds along with an LED (light-emitting) lamp; and finally, an app for your smart phone which controls the entire system and actually provides you with feedback about your overall sleep experience.

Another sleep-related gadget introduced at the electronics show was something called Sleepow, a pillow that plays various tones at slight different frequencies into each ear to promote relaxation conducive to restful sleep.

What is the evidence for it? Though NASA did its own testing and was satisfied enough with the results for its light color system before spending money to develop it, there hasn't been enough time for quality studies to be done and published showing the sleep benefits to consumers of these other technologies. So in the meantime, buyer beware. With that caution in mind, it sure wouldn't hurt to try out these devices if you can afford them. Over time as the gadgets compete in the marketplace, their prices will probably come down sufficiently so they become more affordable for most people.

Qigong

What is it? You may have some trouble pronouncing the word Qigong ('chi-kung'), but beyond the name, anyone can benefit from this ancient Chinese practice because it uses your body posture, your breathing, and your ability to create visualizations to activate your general health maintenance and to treat a variety of health conditions, including insomnia.

Any of you readers can learn the practice of Qigong to maintain or improve your health. Medical experts in Qigong can be found on the Internet who will walk you through the basic steps of how to begin a Qigong practice. These websites can also tell you where to turn to for professional guidance and training. You may even undertake the ancient practice only to decide that you wish to deepen your experience of it by taking it to another level.

What is the evidence for it? Few medical studies have been done on the usefulness of a Qigong practice for enhancing sleep quality. One study was performed on perimenopausal (the beginning of the estrogen decline leading to menopause) women with good results.

In this June 2012 study published in the *Journal of Alternative and Complementary Medicine*, a group of 70 women aged 45 years and above who were experiencing menopausal symptoms did a 12-week, 30-minute-a-day session of Qigong. They were monitored over this period for all aspects of their sleep experience. At the conclusion of the study the scientists found that "the longer a person practiced this form of meditative exercise, the greater the improvement in sleeping quality."

Dozens of medical studies have demonstrated Qigong's benefits in other realms of health and healing. Its overall potential is illustrated by a case detailed in a 2004 issue of *The Journal of Alternative and Complementary Medicine*, written by two medical professors at the University of Medicine and Dentistry of New Jersey. A 58-year-old Caucasian man suffered from a series of chronic conditions, including high prostate-specific antigen (PSA) levels, asthma, edema in his legs, and allergies. After several months of daily intensive Qigong therapy, the researchers found that "the patient discontinued all medications (8 in total) and lost 35 pounds; his blood pressure dropped from 220/110 with medication to 120/75 without medication (in 2 weeks); pulse rate dropped; the edema in his legs went away; symptoms of asthma or allergies disappeared; the PSA level dropped from 11 to 4 (normal), all without any medications."

Yoga

What is it? Don't be fooled by what you thought you knew about it. Yoga isn't just a series of movements that some people use for exercise, and it isn't just a spiritual practice used by New Agers trying to find bliss. Yoga means 'union', and that's exactly what practitioners of yoga attempt to do—unite their mind and body and spirit through movement to enhance their overall vitality and maintain their health.

Since at least the second century B.C., when oral and written records indicate that yoga first came about as a mind-body system of health in India, its physical postures and breathing exercises have been regarded by its practitioners through the ensuing centuries as having a positive impact on their overall health.

You should probably experiment to choose a style of yoga practice that best suits your physical condition and health needs. Yoga experts online and associated with yoga studios can describe simple breath control exercises, called pranayamas, to aid digestion and sleep induction.

The basic body postures and movements in yoga, known as asanas, are described in yoga reference sources, along with information on how your mind is utilized to bring focus and awareness to the practice. These reference sources can be found on the Internet so you can embrace a style of yoga practice in more depth using widely available educational books and videos, including YouTube.

What is the evidence for it? From 30% up to 90% of cancer survivors report impaired sleep. A lot of compelling research has been done looking at whether yoga can reduce pain and improve sleep quality in cancer patients.

For example, a September 2013 study in the *Journal of Clinical Oncology* reported how 410 cancer survivors experiencing sleep disruption were assigned either to a control group (not using yoga) or to a group doing a four-week yoga class. Most of the study participants were women recovering from breast cancer. The style of yoga they used was Hatha combined with breathing exercises and meditation. The volunteers in the yoga group, said the study authors, "demonstrated greater improvements in sleep quality, subjective sleep quality, daytime dysfunction, wake after sleep onset, sleep efficiency, and {lower} medication use at post intervention compared with standard care participants."

An Exercise For Pain and Sleeplessness

With the permission of psychotherapist Donald Altman, the author of many inspirational self-help books, including *The Mindfulness Code, The Joy Compass,* and *One-Minute Mindfulness,* I am giving you access to two scripts that he uses in guided mediations to induce relaxation. These can be useful in dealing with both pain conditions and insomnia and sleeplessness.

You can utilize these exercises either by reading the script and following its directions, or you can tape the script using your own or someone else's voice and then play it back just before trying to sleep.

SCRIPT ONE: Guided Sleep Relaxation Exercise

Donald Altman: Insomnia is a problem that affects many people. Sometimes we're so over stimulated from caffeine and our daily worries that we go to bed with our minds racing and our body wound up tight. This meditation will help. First, though, be aware of your daily caffeine intake. Caffeine can stay in the body for up to 36 hours, and it is in coffee and soda, and chocolate. If you have more than 1.5 grams of caffeine daily, then you need to take action and slowly cut down.

One more tip about sleep. Your body sets a sleep rhythm to the light with melatonin. That means that when you sleep, your room needs to be dark. If there is light coming in from outside or from another room, then your body may not set your sleep clock.

...we go to bed with our minds racing and our body wound up tight.

Also, you can drink some warm milk or chamomile tea at bedtime, which has known properties to create relaxation. Drinking this tea can be a ritual for you at bedtime. Don't leave the TV on until the last minute. Some soothing music and tea could help create a new bedtime ritual. Reading in bed may actually keep you awake longer. So save the reading for before you go to bed, and make sure the bedroom is quiet.

Before starting, take three deep breaths to prepare you for this sleep relaxation. Take one breath to release tension, one to release emotion, and one just for the fun of it.

This sleep relaxation practice consists of two parts. The first part will help release your body's muscular tension. The second part will relax your mind.

For the first part, you will tense and relax the various parts of your body, beginning from your feet and move slowly up to your head and face. Have you ever done isometrics? This is a lot like that.

While you're lying down, tense up your toes and soles of your feet for at least 10 seconds. Try it now, and count slowly to 10. Don't strain so hard that you hurt yourself. You're just tensing up so you can feel the muscles. Now when you reach 10, immediately let the toes and soles of your feet relax completely. Feel how different and relaxing it is to feel no tension in your feet.

Spend the next 15 seconds or even half a minute focusing on what it feels like as each muscle group relaxes. If you want, you can even say to yourself something like "all the tension in my feet is gone, my stress is slipping away and dissolving, I am really enjoying this feeling of deep relaxation and peace."

As with any mindfulness practice, if your mind starts to wander, gently bring it back to each body group as you tense the muscles, and then quickly release them. Now, I'll lead you through this exercise.

> *You probably want to lie down, and tighten your ankles on both legs. Count to 10 as you feel all the muscles and tendons become stiff and tight. As you do this, keep all your other muscle groups—such as your legs and arms—relaxed. There, now let go. Feel how your ankles get soft, how the tension and stress are gone. Feel this completely, how your skin is relaxed, and the tissues deep in the ankle are free from any tension.*
>
> *Now, tighten your leg muscles including your thighs and knees. Feel all the muscles, even those you weren't aware of before. Let them expand as they tense. They may grow tired and fatigued, but keep them as tense as you can. Now at the count of 10, let them go.*
>
> *Total relaxation, total freedom from tension, these legs that work so hard to support you during the day are now at peace, relieved of their hard work and given permission to rest...deep down into the knee and leg muscles. Enjoy this feeling of relaxation.*
>
> *Next, moving up the body, tense the buttocks and pelvic region. Tighten as much as you can, holding it without*

straining too much. Feel how much tension there is, how many muscles there are. Even the tension that exists in your skeleton, feel that too. Now, relax totally, completely.

Let this section of your body be free from stress, let the muscles go, let their tension drain out of you until this part of your body is relaxed and calm. Let yourself enjoy this sensation of no tension.

Now, tense your abdomen and the muscles behind it in your lower back. Let this whole section tighten, even tightening the muscles at the side of your abdomen. Notice how this makes it hard for you to breathe. Now, after 10 seconds, let this tightness release completely.

How nice it is to breathe freely, to have your muscles in your lower back, even your spine, free from tension. Let yourself enjoy your body as it lets go of this rigidity and becomes loose and peaceful.

Moving up the body, tense your chest and upper back muscles. Hold them tightly, tightly, feeling how constricted they can be. As you do this, continue to breathe into your belly. Feel the tightness even in your rib cage and back, how your shoulder blades feel tense.

Now let it go. Feel how quickly the tension lets go. Release it from your body and feel how so much of your body, from your toes to your chest, is now relaxed and calm.

Now, tighten your fists hard. Feel how the tightness extends into your fingers and into your wrists. This is what it is like to fight with daily tensions, all clenched up and nervous and strained. Does this feel familiar to you? Now, at the count of 10, release it all. Let your fingers, your knuckles, and wrists relax and open. Feel the blood flow back in, and feel what it is like to not live with yourself clenched and straining. Feel the tension leave each finger; let it out like steam from a teapot. See the energy leaving like trails of steam rising from each fingertip…until there is no strain, no tension or clenching left.

Now tighten your biceps and elbows together, feeling all the muscles grow larger and tighter. As you do this, your hands hang, still completely relaxed. Hold for 10, then releasing all the tension in your biceps and elbows. Let your arms fall at your side, and feel the difference when you let the energy go. Just experience them like this for a few more moments.

Now, you can straighten your arms out and tighten the triceps, the muscle on the back of your arm that opposes the biceps. Again, feel what it is like to clench and become rigid with this body group as you count to 10. Feel the fatigue, the extension of the muscle into your arm.

When you relax, let your arm fall, feeling the joy of letting go of this tension. There is no need to hold on to the tension, your muscles want to relax.

Next, your neck and upper shoulders get tight as possible without straining. Feel how they carry so much tension. Hold this until the count of 10. Relax immediately, letting the tension flow out, feeling your neck muscles and shoulders surrender to the feeling and peace that they have from there being no tightness. Relax them even more deeply, letting your neck and shoulders sink more deeply into the floor or bed or wherever you are lying down.

Now, you are going to tense and tighten your entire face and skull. If you could, try to make a fist with your face, tightening your eyes, scrunching up your cheeks, and at the same time, you feel your jaws open wider. Your lips are tight even though your mouth is open. Even feel your ears and scalp tighten and draw back. You didn't know you had so many muscles in your face, but now you feel them all, tight and fatigued.

At the count of 10, release them all, as you imagine your entire head and face growing smooth and long…your eyelids and eyebrows relaxing, your mouth and jaw letting go. All the skin on your face feels totally smooth and relaxed, with the sensation of deep tranquility, like it has had a gentle massage. Your ears and skull are free from any tension at all. Any remaining tension leaves your head and face, and now your whole body is relaxed, at rest, tension free.

Spend a few moments enjoying this feeling. There is no need to be tense now, because this is your time to rest, and you can lead yourself through this body relaxation any time you want.

After you complete this muscle relaxation, you can follow up by doing the mental relaxation for sleep. With each breath you take, you'll mentally repeat a word with each out-breath that will help you sleep. I suggest the use of a soothing word such as "calm," "peace," "relax," or "love" to relax you while focusing on your breath. You can still use one of those words, or, you might try the word "sleep." Or you could say the word "rest" or even "restful sleep." If your mind wanders, just bring it back by simply noticing your breath as you set your intention to create and end each breath.

And, if you want, you can alter the muscle relaxation to tighten and relax various parts of the face instead of the entire face at once. Feel free to alter the routine and find something that flows for you. I hope this sleep relaxation is useful. Stick with it, and set your intention for a restful sleep before you even walk into the bedroom.

SCRIPT TWO: Using a Nighttime Calming Word to Quiet a Racing, Anxious Mind

Donald Altman: The words you place your attention have a lot to do with shaping the inner well-being circuitry of your brain, as well as the outer circuitry of your sleep behavior. The practice we're going to learn now—of focusing on a calming word to invite balance and quickly calm your emotions—is especially good when your mind feels turbulent, overactive, anxious, or negative.

Centering your attention in the now moment using breath and a word is a wonderful way to quiet the mind, to quell anxiety and stress, and to build concentration. Let's try it right now.

To begin, you'll want to choose a word or short phrase that you can focus on and repeat in your mind, over and over. The words or phrases you can use for this practice are infinite. You could, for example, mentally repeat words such as "restful sleep," "one," "quiet mind," "peace," "shalom," or "now." You might even decide to use a prayer, such as the ancient Jesus Prayer, "Lord Jesus Christ, have mercy upon me."

Feel free to get creative and use words that feel good. For example, I know an avid golfer who finds the phrase "bogey free" to be calming and helpful for him. If the word you are using doesn't feel right, you can always try another one next time.

It's also a good idea to avoid words that associate you with a particular memory. If you find that a word stimulates memory or intrudes by creating more thoughts, you can choose a more neutral word. Even using a neutral word like "one" has been shown to lower stress.

The purpose of this practice is to release stress and gently quiet your mind by turning it away from the turbulence or racing mind that many people experience at night when trying to sleep. You can think of this practice as dropping a pebble into rushing water. The word you focus on will gently take you beneath the choppy surface to where there are no waves…and your mind and thoughts will settle down and grow quiet in the stillness beneath the waves. You can also imagine this practice as a way of calming the surface so you can float on top of the still water.

This practice can be done either during the day to calm the mind,or at night to help you sleep.

Now, whether sitting or lying down, close your eyes. While repeating your word, you will be placing about 10 or 15 percent of your awareness on the breath. Make sure you breathe evenly, and into the belly. As you think of your word, you do not have to concentrate hard. This is not about forcing or creating too much effort. Think of this as a gentle and effortless way of floating on the top of the water, or slowly settling in the stillness beneath the water.

Imagine that you are just preferring or favoring your chosen word over other thoughts. If your mind wanders off into thinking about the past or the future for a while, that's okay. Even if you get drowsy, that's okay, too. Just allow yourself to gently return to your word again.

Sometimes, it may feel like your word has gone inward, as if it's still there even though you're not repeating it. If this happens, simply allow yourself to experience it this way. Your other senses may also intrude as you repeat your word. You may hear a noise or you may feel a sensation in your body. Don't push these away; rather, just notice them and return to the breath and the word.

Strong feelings or emotions may occur while you are repeating your word.

If you experience a strong negative feeling, see what it is like to sit with it until it passes. Your mind will naturally be drawn to it, and you don't need to explain or understand it, but let yourself notice if it increases or lessens in intensity. If for any reason it doesn't dissolve away and you get uncomfortable, you can always stop the practice by opening your eyes, distracting yourself, or just resting. Know that you can always return to this practice later.

At other times, you may experience an uplifting feeling while doing this practice. Whatever your experience may be today, the next practice session may bring totally different feelings. Give yourself permission to be open to whatever arises.

I like to think of this as a gentle practice, so if you feel the need to shift your position on the ground or chair or bed, go ahead and do so—but do so with full awareness.

(You can visit Donald Altman's http://www.mindfulnesscode. com to find his books and CDs discussing various aspects of mindfulness practices. Also his CD *Healing, Relaxation and Stress Reduction* is only available on his www.mindfulpractices.com website.)